WELFARE STATE AMERICA

WELFARE STATE AMERICA

Safety Net or Social Contract?

MICHAEL KRONENWETTER

An Impact Book

FRANKLIN WATTS

NEW YORK • CHICAGO • LONDON • TORONTO • SYDNEY

Photographs copyright©: Archive Photos/American Stock: pp. 1, 3, 4 bottom; The Bettmann Archive: pp. 2, 6; Photo Researchers, Inc.: pp. 4 top, 16 (Michael Uffer); UPI/Bettmann Newsphotos: pp. 5, 7 top, 8 top, 9, 13; AP/ Wide World Photos: pp. 7 bottom, 10; Impact Visuals: pp. 8 bottom (Ken Martin), 11 (Jim West), 14 (George Cohen); United Nations/P. Sudhakaran: p. 12; The Welfare Warriors, Milwaukee, WI: p. 15.

Library of Congress Cataloging-in-Publication Data

Kronenwetter, Michael.
    Welfare state America : safety net or social contract? / Michael Kronenwetter.
        p.   cm.—(Impact book)
    Includes bibliographical references and index.
    Summary: Examines the welfare system in the United States from its inception during the 1930s to the present, discussing its various programs, problems that have occurred, and efforts to reform it.
    ISBN 0-531-13010-X
    1. Human services—United States—History—20th century.
    2. Public welfare—United States—History—20th century.
    [1. Public welfare—History.   2. Human services—History.]
    I. Title.
HV91.K77   1992
361.973—dc20   92-35880   CIP   AC

CONTENTS

PROLOGUE

9   The "Other America"

CHAPTER ONE

13   What Is a Welfare State?

CHAPTER TWO

17   "To Promote the General Welfare"

CHAPTER THREE

31   The Birth of the Welfare State

CHAPTER FOUR

41   The Development of the American Welfare State

CHAPTER FIVE

57   Social Security: Foundation of the Welfare State

CHAPTER SIX
67 Major Federal Welfare Programs

CHAPTER SEVEN
75 Living on Welfare

CHAPTER EIGHT
83 The Welfare State Debate

CHAPTER NINE
95 The Need for Reform

CHAPTER TEN
101 Ideas for Reform

113 SOURCE NOTES

121 BIBLIOGRAPHY

125 INDEX

A decent provision for the poor is the true test of civilization.

— SAMUEL JOHNSON

I don't think our democracy can be the example that it wants to be unless we make it work better for the people who have been left behind in the American dream we talk about.

— JACK KEMP, Secretary of Housing
and Urban Development

The "Other America"

AN eighty-year-old woman in Cleveland, Ohio, falls in her kitchen. A terrible pain seizes her when she tries to twist her legs under her to rise to her feet. Her husband, who is too frail to lift her from the floor, calls an ambulance and she is taken to the hospital. X rays reveal that her hip is broken.

The doctors decide that if they don't operate, she will be crippled for life. The operation is successful, but the woman requires a long stay in the hospital, and an even longer period of rehabilitation after that.

The hospital bill comes to more than $15,000. The fees of the doctors, anesthetists, physical therapists, and other medical professionals add up to thousands of dollars more. In addition, there are charges for the ambulance, and high costs for drugs, for a walker, and for other physical supports and devices she will need in order to walk comfortably again.

The woman and her husband have no savings, and live on an income of less than $1,000 a month. They can pay only a tiny fraction of the enormous costs brought about by her fall. The rest is paid by Medicare, a government program that helps pay medical expenses for elderly people who qualify.

A sixth-grade boy in Boise, Idaho, leaves home for school without eating breakfast. His mother deserted the family shortly after he was born, and his father recently lost his job at the car wash down the street. The job never paid enough to save up against this kind of financial disaster, so the family has very little money. Until the father finds a new job, or his unemployment insurance kicks in, the family budget will not provide more than one meal a day for either of them.

The boy, at least, will get two meals today. At lunchtime, the school will serve him a meal that is hot and nutritious, if not very tasty. It will be provided to him, free of charge to his family, by a government-funded school lunch program.

Like many other lonely people, a middle-aged man in Sarasota, Florida, listens to the radio every evening. He likes the call-in shows the most, and thinks of the hosts and regular callers as friends. They keep him company.

Turning the radio off is the very last thing the man does each night before going to bed. He never turns off the lights in his tiny apartment, because he doesn't have to. Except when he's had company, they've never been on. He has no use for them. The man has been blind since his eyes were scalded in a chemical accident at the plant where he worked.

The economic effects of his injury have been almost as disastrous as the physical ones. In the five years since the accident happened, he has been unable to find another job. He's had to give up the four-room apartment in which he'd lived for decades, and move into this one-bedroom efficiency he lives in now. He could not afford even this, if it were not for the money he gets each month from the Supplemental Security Income program for the blind.

The eighteen-year-old mother in Minneapolis is alarmed to see the snow swirling outside her apartment window. It looks like a real snowstorm, the kind that snarls traffic, and makes the sidewalks treacherous with ice. *Oh no*, she thinks, *I'm already late, now this will make me even later.*

Her six-month-old daughter was up with colic most of the night, and so the mother has only managed to catch a few hours' sleep. Now she has overslept, and the job interview is in half an hour.

She quickly puts on her best dress, and makes herself as presentable as she can in the short time she dares to steal to apply her makeup and comb her hair. Then she bundles her baby in a blanket, grabs her coat, and heads out the door. Thankful that the baby is still soundly asleep after her exhausting night of crying, the young woman leaves her with a neighbor and heads out into the blizzard.

Walking against the icy wind, it takes ten minutes longer than expected to reach the department store whose ad for clerks she had seen in the paper the night before. Her face stung raw with the cold, her makeup ruined, she rushes through the aisles toward the personnel office. But before she gets there, she is met by a line of young women like herself coming in the opposite direction. "You here for the jobs, honey?" one asks her kindly. "You're too late. They're already filled."

That's the way it's been for the young woman, ever since her parents kicked her out of their home when they found out she was pregnant. Without even a high school diploma, she has been unable to find any job at all. If it wasn't for the little money she and her baby get each month from the government Aid to Families with Dependent Children program, they would be homeless.

The situations described above are typical of the realities faced by millions of Americans with limited incomes who receive benefits from government programs. All these people rely on the government to help them meet the basic necessities of life in a modern world. To the extent that it does so, the government of the United States has taken on the role of a welfare state.

What Is a
Welfare State?

THE United States entered the 1990s
with more than 33.6 million of its people living in poverty.
According to the official estimate of the U.S. Census Bureau, roughly 13.5 percent of all Americans were poor—
and their numbers were growing fast.[1]

For the first time since the Great Depression, homelessness had become a major, growing problem in every
region of the country. Requests for emergency shelter rose
24 percent in 1990, while requests for food aid jumped 22
percent.[2] In the winter of 1991–92, a Salvation Army official in Michigan reported that people were appealing to
the Army in "numbers we've never experienced before . . .
we could open fifty [new] shelters and fill them."[3]

Even by the Census Bureau's estimates, roughly one
out of every seven men, women, and children in the United
States is poor. But many critics complain that even that
shockingly high percentage is misleadingly low. "Whatever figures [the government gives out] will understate the
degree of poverty in the country today," charged Robert
Greenstein, the director of a liberal research organization
called the Center on Budget and Policy Priorities.[4]

Critics like Greenstein base their charge on the way
the government defines poverty. In 1991, for example, the

government defined poverty for an unmarried adult as an income under $6,125. For a family of four, it was $13,359. The poverty level for elderly Americans was set even lower, at $5,671.

The specific figures change from year to year, but the critics argue that they are always unrealistically low. They point out that there are few places in the country where families or individuals of any age can get by on incomes that small, and claim that a more realistic definition of poverty would place the number of poor Americans at least 45 million.[5]

Although about two thirds of poor people are white, the poverty rate for minorities is higher than for whites. African Americans have the highest rate of all, 32 percent. Roughly 12 percent of elderly white Americans, and 32 percent of elderly African Americans, are poor.

But children are the poorest Americans of all. For the first time since poverty figures have been kept, a higher proportion of children are poor than members of any other age group. Just about one out of every five American children—19.6 percent—is poor. The rate for very young children is even higher, 22.5 percent. For minority children, things are even worse: 36.2 percent of all Latino children and a staggering 43.7 percent of African-American children fall under the official definition of poverty.[6] Estimates of the number of poor children who are homeless range from 273,000 (U.S. Department of Education) to 500,000 (National Coalition for the Homeless).[7]

A surprisingly large number of poor people work. A government study covering the years 1983 to 1987 showed that roughly one out of every six poor children lived in a family whose head was employed full time.[8] Even many of the homeless poor are employed. A survey in Washington State revealed that roughly one-fifth to one-quarter of the people in homeless shelters there were actually employed more than twenty hours a week.[9]

* * *

Like the people described in the Prologue, each of the 33 to 45 million poor people in the United States is an individual human being. A woman, man, or child, with the same needs and rights as every other American.

Over the years, an elaborate system of social programs and agencies has grown up to assist these people, and to keep others from joining them in poverty. There are scores of such programs, some run by the federal government, and some by state or local governments. They fall into several different categories, and are called by a bewildering variety of names: welfare, Social Security, entitlements, general assistance, public assistance, unemployment insurance, veterans' benefits, Medicaid, Medicare, food stamps.

Each has different provisions, and provides a different kind or amount of assistance. But they all have the same general purpose. They help Americans achieve their basic economic needs: food, shelter, clothing, education, health care, and the means to survive in a modern society. Some, like Social Security, are designed to help virtually all Americans meet some minimum standard of well-being. Others, like unemployment insurance, are designed to help people meet some unexpected economic crisis in their lives.

Taken together, these programs, and the agencies that run them, make up the American social welfare system. This system is often compared to an economic safety net: a complex web of measures, strung together to keep people from falling too deeply into poverty and despair.

By developing these programs, the United States has transformed itself into a welfare state—that is, a nation that assumes the responsibility for meeting the fundamental economic needs of its people.

Historian Arthur Schlesinger, Jr., defines the welfare state as "a system wherein government agrees to underwrite certain levels of employment, income, education, medical aid, social security, and housing for all its citizens." The government does not necessarily supply all these requirements itself. It often encourages the private sector—individuals, businesses, charitable organizations —to create and distribute them. "But," as Schlesinger explains, "it does accept the ultimate responsibility of guaranteeing 'floors' in certain crucial areas, below which it conceives tolerable living to be impossible."[10]

By this definition, virtually every economically developed country in the world is a welfare state, and almost every underdeveloped country is working to become one. In general, the more developed the country is, the higher the level of services it guarantees to its people.

Welfare states come in many varieties, with every possible kind of government and economic system. Some welfare states are democratic, some are totalitarian. Some are capitalist, some are socialist. What sets them apart is only their commitment to assure certain goods and services to their people.

Different welfare states provide drastically different levels of benefits. Some satisfy themselves with a safety net of services, available only to those with special needs, such as orphans, the elderly, workers who lose their jobs, the sick, or the disabled. Others supply a wide range of benefits to everyone, regardless of his or her individual circumstances.

The purest form of welfare state would guarantee comfortable, safe housing; a nutritious and filling diet; birth-to-adult education; cradle-to-grave health care; and at least a minimum income to every man, woman, and child in the country. The United States is a long way from being that kind of welfare state.

What kind of welfare state is the United States? How did the American version of the welfare state evolve? What does it provide, and what doesn't it? What are the arguments for and against the present social welfare system, and what might be done to improve that system in the future?

"To Promote the General Welfare"

THE American welfare state did not just happen. It grew out of the country's history, and out of the ways different generations of Americans responded to changing social conditions. It was formed out of their often changing attitudes toward work, charity, and the role of government.

In many ways, the modern welfare state still reflects many of these old attitudes: attitudes that still color the way we think about welfare and the people who receive it.

The Constitution

In the Preamble to the Constitution, the country's founders declared that they were acting "to form a more perfect Union, establish Justice, ensure domestic Tranquility, provide for the common defense, promote the general welfare, and secure the Blessings of Liberty to ourselves and our Posterity."

From the very beginning, then, the "general welfare" was accepted as a basic concern of government. The founders put it on a par with such traditional American values as Justice and Liberty as a major reason for having a national government at all.

And yet, the United States did not start out to be a welfare state in the modern sense of the term. The concept of "welfare" was understood very differently in the eighteenth century than it is today. The emphasis then was on the adjective "general." For the first century and more of the nation's history, the government promoted the "general welfare" mostly by encouraging economic activity and westward expansion.

In practice, this often meant that government policies were designed to promote American industry and trade. As the nation spread across the continent, the government took steps to ensure settlement in the West, and commerce between the West and the original states. It encouraged the building of the great roads, canals, and railroads that made commerce possible.

The great transcontinental railroads were made almost immediately profitable by the government's gifts of huge tracts of lands to the railroad companies. Those companies, in turn, parcelled out the land to farmers and town builders to encourage settlement along their rights of way. Great tracts of land were handed out free to anyone who would live and work on them for a given period of time. The homesteaders who took the government up on this offer attracted hordes of entrepreneurs who followed them west. Within a century, these new settlers had established farms and ranches, built towns, and founded businesses all the way across the continent.

A New Class of Poor People

The nineteenth century was a time of enormous growth for the American economy. There were occasional crises—recessions, depressions, and even the terrible disruption of the Civil War—but overall the economy churned along at a terrific rate. The industrial revolution transformed the economy, bringing about a host of major new social and economic developments that created the conditions that eventually led to the formation of the welfare state.

One of the major factors in the enormous economic development was the big business corporation. Huge new companies sprang up almost overnight in basic industries like coal and steel, transportation and manufacturing.

The people who owned and ran these companies prospered almost beyond belief. Many tradespeople, retailers, and professional people prospered as well. The number of successful, well-off Americans was growing at an unprecedented rate. But the number of poor people was growing, too. In fact, a whole new class of poor Americans was being formed.

The typical worker in a nineteenth-century factory labored six or seven days a week, ten or twelve hours a day, and received only starvation wages in return. Working conditions were unhealthy, exhausting, and extremely dangerous. The physical hazards were made worse by the likelihood that workers would lose their jobs if they were ever injured or fell sick. In fact, any worker could be fired at any time, for any reason, or for no reason at all.

Before long, America's cities were swelling with hordes of the working poor and the unemployed. They huddled together in fire-trap tenements, in neighborhoods that became slums almost as soon as they were built. On one side of town, millions of laborers and their families struggled desperately to survive on wages of a dollar or two a day. On the other, shiploads of hopeful new immigrants were landing on American shores, eager to work for even that, or to find a piece of land on which to set up a farm.

For the most part, the government ignored the growing class of industrial poor. Despite its duty to promote the general welfare, the federal government did nothing to help them. Nor did it do anything to help the thousands of immigrant farmers who failed to make their homesteads produce enough food to feed themselves. Nor did it help any of the other Americans who faced serious financial or health problems.

Most nineteenth-century Americans would probably have been outraged by the idea that the government *might* help these people. Charity, most people felt, was not the government's job. The "general welfare" might be a concern of government, but the welfare of individuals was not.

Social Darwinism

At the root of nineteenth-century attitudes toward welfare was the way people believed the economy operated. Then, as now, the American economy was essentially capitalist. That is, people invested their private capital—their money —in various businesses. The businesses competed to produce and sell goods and services. When the businesses made money, the capitalists took that money in the form of profits. When the businesses lost money, the capitalists lost the money they'd invested.

In theory, this system was good for everyone. The capitalists' businesses produced goods and employed workers, thus increasing the overall wealth of society. The competition between capitalists helped to assure the best possible goods at the lowest possible prices. If one company was charging too much, or selling shoddy goods, consumers could always buy from a competitor.

In practice, however, this system worked out much better for successful capitalist investors than it did for anyone else. The tycoons who ran the massive new business corporations accumulated fabulous wealth and power for themselves. Some—like John D. Rockefeller, who controlled Standard Oil, and Andrew Carnegie of Carnegie Steel—managed to seize personal control of whole industries. Most of these men (there were no women among them) paid little attention to laws or morality when it came to the way they ran their businesses. They acted with such free-booting ruthlessness that critics called them the "robber barons."

Their arrogance is illustrated by two remarks made by members of the Vanderbilt family, who controlled the New York Railroad. The first was Commodore Cornelius Vanderbilt's response to a lawyer who warned him that one of his schemes was against the law. "What do I care about the law?" he asked. "Hain't I got the power?" The second was his son William's even more brazen declaration: "The public be damned."[1]

The robber barons seemed to care very little about the people who worked for them, or bought their products. They set wages low and prices high. The products they produced were often defective, and even dangerous. Workers who tried to organize unions were beaten up or fired. Sometimes those who continued to cause trouble were killed. Meanwhile, the competition that was supposed to keep prices down and quality up often didn't exist. The most successful tycoons soon crushed, or simply bought out, competing businesses.

The federal government did little to protect either workers, consumers, or competitors from the robber barons' power. For the most part, nineteenth-century corporations were allowed to operate without regulation by the government. This policy of not interfering in the affairs of private business came to be known by the French expression *laissez-faire*, meaning "to leave alone."

There was a general sense that what was good for business was good for America, and for the American *people* as well. After all, it was believed that business drove the American economy—and it was the economy that put food on everyone's table and a roof over everyone's head.

In reality, however, not everyone *had* food or a roof. While the most successful capitalists became fantastically rich, and millions of other Americans prospered, many millions of other people had to struggle just to stay alive. Some of them worked in the factories run by the big business corporations, some worked on the land, while others could find no work at all. Still others were sick or crippled. No amount of business activity pulled these people out of poverty.

How could a government committed to the general welfare allow such unfair conditions to exist for so many of the people? A new economic theory was invented to provide an answer. It was called Social Darwinism, after the British naturalist Charles Darwin. It was Darwin who had observed that animal species competed with each other for available resources. He theorized that the stronger, most adaptable species would win that competition and survive. The weaker ones would lose, and eventually die out in a process he called "natural selection," or "survival of the fittest."

Ultimately, Darwin argued, this competition was good for the animal species. Since the strongest or fittest individuals won out, they were the ones who survived to produce the most offspring. Their offspring inherited the qualities that had made their parents strong. Meanwhile, few of the weak individuals survived to pass their weaknesses on to the next generation. In this way, the species as a whole got stronger with each generation that was born.[2]

Social Darwinists tried to apply this theory to the economy. They argued that competition was a law of nature, and that it applied to economic affairs just as it did to biology. Just as competition for the available natural resources made an animal species strong, they argued, competition for economic wealth made a human society strong. That was because the smartest, strongest, most determined members of society would inevitably win the economic competition, too. They would become the leaders of industry, the capitalists, the tycoons.

In the process, they would accumulate great wealth and power while the weakest members of society would fall into poverty. Because of this competition, the "fittest" people would always be in control of society. It may seem unfair, the Social Darwinists argued, but it was really best for all concerned.

Andrew Carnegie, a poor Scottish immigrant who acquired fabulous wealth as the head of a vast steel empire, expressed it this way: "The price which society pays for the law of competition, like the price it pays for cheap comforts and luxuries, is . . . great; but the advantages of this law are greater still, for it is to this law that we owe our wonderful material development, which brings improved conditions in its train. But, whether the law be benign or not . . . [i]t is here; we cannot evade it; no substitutes for it have been found; and while the law may be sometimes hard on the individual, it is best for the race, because it ensures the survival of the fittest in every department."[3]

Almost everyone who was in business, or who hoped to be, believed in some version of this theory. For many, the belief was hazy and unformed, but there was a general sense that accumulating wealth was a virtue, even when it was done at the expense of other people. These were people who dreamed of being the winners in the great competition for wealth, and Social Darwinism was the philosophy of winners.

Many Social Darwinists felt little sympathy for the poor people who were trampled under in this competition. What did it matter to these winners if the "law of competition" was "hard on the individual"? After all, the only ones who suffered were the failures, the weak members of the species society would be better off without.

Some Social Darwinists even argued that it was a mistake to help the poor in any way. Cushioning the effects of poverty, they said, undermined the law of competition. Hunger, disease, and homelessness were not really evils at all. They were positive goods. They gave people a reason to work as hard as they could to avoid being poor. Relieving the suffering of the poor would only lessen the incentive for them to work hard and be productive. Suffering might strengthen the best of them, but relief could only weaken them.

Some Social Darwinists went even further. They argued, as one analyst put it, that those who could not pull

.nselves out of poverty should "be allowed, nay, be isted, to die."[4]

The Gospel of Wealth and the Social Gospel

Social Darwinism was a kind of economic religion. It provided a moral justification for capitalism, excusing some of what seemed to be capitalism's excesses. The religious nature of Social Darwinism was recognized by its believers and its critics alike. Carnegie, who was one of its leading advocates, even called a small book he wrote about it *The Gospel of Wealth*.

Some Christian religious leaders adopted the "gospel" themselves, preaching it alongside the gospels of the Bible. Great wealth, they argued, was a sign of God's favor, maybe even God's reward for virtue. An Episcopal Bishop named William Lawrence expressed this belief as a matter of faith: "In the long run, it is only to the man of morality that wealth comes," he declared. "Godliness is in league with riches."[5]

Not all American clergymen believed in the so-called Gospel of Wealth. More traditional preachers considered it a parody of the teachings of the Christian religion.

"Here then is the issue," wrote the philosopher Charles S. Pierce in 1893. "The gospel of Christ says that progress comes from every individual merging his individuality in sympathy with his neighbors. On the other side, the conviction of the nineteenth century is that progress takes place by virtue of every individual's striving for himself with all his might and trampling his neighbor under foot whenever he gets a chance to do so. This may accurately be called the Gospel of Greed."[6]

Pierce and several other clergymen who opposed the Gospel of Greed preached what came to be known as the Social Gospel instead. They called on successful people to help those who were less fortunate. Private charity was particularly needed in the nineteenth century, when the federal government did almost nothing to help those in need.

Personal Charity

Private charity came in many forms, and from many sources. Some even came from the robber barons themselves. Unlike other Social Darwinists, Andrew Carnegie believed that the winners in the competition for wealth had a moral duty toward the losers.

The "man of wealth," Carnegie said, was actually "the mere agent and trustee for his poorer brethren." It was his duty to administer the wealth he controlled, not just for himself and his family, but "for the community." The fact that he had accumulated the wealth in the first place assured that he would administer it "far better than [the community] could or would have done for itself."[7]

Several robber barons fulfilled this responsibility by donating huge sums to charity. Carnegie himself gave around $350 million to various projects, including almost 2,800 local libraries, whose books, he said, could be used by talented poor people to help them pull themselves out of poverty—just as he had done. Many of the local libraries in cities and towns around the country today owe their start to Andrew Carnegie. Not all the robber barons were so generous, however, and some ignored their duty as "trustees" altogether.

Although the charitable gifts of Carnegie and the robber barons were sometimes impressive, most nineteenth-century charity was given out by ordinary Americans. Much of it was highly personal—a neighbor helping a neighbor, or lending a hand to a stranger in need.

Out in the countryside, in particular, people often had to rely on their friends and neighbors in times of trouble. Most were more than willing to help out when they could. Almost everyone in rural America, on the farms and the frontier alike, had been through hard times themselves. They knew what it was like.

For those whose friends and neighbors were kindhearted and generous, personal charity had some great advantages. The help they received was usually immediate, and was specifically designed to meet their needs. A hungry man got food. A family who'd lost their home got a barn to sleep in that night. A young girl with nothing to wear on her feet was given a luckier child's hand-me-down shoes.

But not everyone had kindhearted neighbors. And even those who were lucky enough to receive help couldn't rely on it. The hungry child who received an apple from a kindly neighbor today might be refused one tomorrow. The poor were totally dependent on the whims of those more fortunate than themselves.

The Urban Poor and the Growth of Organized Charity

In many ways, the city poor were worse off than the poor in the countryside. And, as the nineteenth century moved on, there were more and more of them. Many of the urban poor were immigrants, whose numbers were growing in the cities at an unprecedented rate. For most of the century, they were encouraged to come to America by a government eager to find laborers for America's new industries and settlers to populate the West.

Typically, they arrived on the docks with few if any contacts in America. Most of the people they met were as poor, bewildered, and desperate as themselves. Political organizations, known as machines, helped out a bit in return for their votes and support, but for the most part they were on their own.

Many of these immigrants, or their descendants, eventually prospered in America. (Andrew Carnegie, himself, was an immigrant.) But, for most of them, success would be a long time away. For many, it would not be themselves, but their children, or their grandchildren, who would finally succeed in America.

In the meantime, they flooded into the poor neighborhoods of the nation's cities, filling them to overflowing. By the mid-nineteenth century, urban slums were growing like poisonous mushrooms. The slum-dwellers lived in terrible conditions. Families of ten or twelve people were often crammed into single rooms in fire-trap tenements. The lightless streets swarmed with orphans, drunks, and drug addicts of both sexes. Children and cripples begged. Desperate men lurked in the shadows of darkened buildings, watching for someone to rob. Women stood on streetcorners, eager to sell themselves for a drink.

The "gospel of wealth" gave no comfort to such people. Nor did the government, which considered the welfare of the urban poor to be none of its business. But the ministers, priests, rabbis, and laymen who believed in the Social Gospel tried to do what they could; and so did many other compassionate Americans.

By the turn of the century, tens of thousands of charitable organizations had sprung up in cities across the country.[8] For the most part, they were designed to relieve the suffering of the urban poor and to help those caught in the snares of addiction to drugs, alcohol, or other vices. Many were made up of volunteers who worked with the poor and suffering for religious reasons, or out of a strong sense of personal compassion.

Most of the organizations were local. They were so small that they could only help a handful of people at a time. Typically, each confined itself to helping a particular group of people, or combatting a specific social evil. Some, like the Belgian Benevolence Society, and the Committee for Ameliorating the Condition of Russian Refugees, worked to help a single ethnic group. Others concentrated on a single vice. The Erring Women's Refuge helped women of the streets, for example, while the Boston Industrial Aid Society helped alcoholics.

A few, though, were big enough to help thousands of people. The largest of them all was the Salvation Army, a British religious and charitable organization that crossed the Atlantic to launch an assault on American poverty in 1880. Its first U.S. branch was in New York City. By the turn of the century, it had 23,000 men and women fighting on the front lines of the battle against poverty and despair—the slums of the nation's big cities.[9]

Much smaller, but almost as influential, was Hull House, a settlement house or neighborhood charity, established by Jane Addams in Chicago in 1889. It quickly became a model for other settlement houses in urban neighborhoods across the country.[10]

The "Deserving" and "Undeserving" Poor

Those who received private charity often had to pay a high psychological price for it. In the first place, many often had to plead to get it. At best, this was a public confession of personal failure. At worst, it was a terrible humiliation.

Many charity-givers made harsh judgments about those they helped. The ones who believed, along with Bishop Lawrence, that "In the long run . . . wealth is in league with Godliness," naturally suspected that poverty was in league with sin.

This belief fit in with what has been called the Protestant work ethic. This is the idea that work is a moral good, and hard work is a virtue in itself. This was a widespread belief in nineteenth-century America, and is summed up in the old saying, "Idle hands are the devil's playthings." If hard work is a sign of a good person, then no work at all must be a sign of a bad one.

No one argued that every wealthy person was good, or that every poor person was immoral. But in the long run, many Americans believed, wealth and poverty were good indications of a person's character. The historian Ralph Henry Gabriel described that belief this way: "For the individual [poverty] was, or at least could be, a transient state. It was a blessing in disguise to the one who rose above it, but to him who did not, it was a symbol of shame, a sort of scarlet letter proclaiming that he was wanting in ability or character, or both."[11]

Many charities would only help those they considered "deserving." That category usually included orphaned children, widows, and disabled veterans. Some groups broadened the definition to include hardworking laborers whose families were too large for them to support, no matter how hard they worked.

Others in need were often assumed to be undeserving wretches who had brought their misfortunes on themselves through drunkenness or other immoral behavior. Most nineteenth-century charities were only willing to help them if they confessed their sins and promised to reform. But many suffering people were either unable or unwilling to reform.

Others, who had no sins to confess in the first place, were not willing to face the humiliation of begging for help. They were too proud to ask for charity, or even to take it when it was offered. Both the proud and the "undeserving" were usually left to fend for themselves.

But even the most "deserving" poor could never really count on help. Although many nineteenth-century charities were noble organizations, the help they provided was hit-and-miss at best. Although each was designed to help only a particular group of people, most were too small to help even all of those in their target groups. What's more, each was only designed to help in one or two particular ways. Most of the poor had many different problems at once. What's more, many of the people who needed help the most didn't qualify for aid from any charity at all.

This situation continued well into the twentieth century. Even after many foreign governments began taking responsibility to improve the condition of their poor, the

United States remained stubbornly committed to laissez-faire. Because of the deeply held belief in the virtues of capitalism and Social Darwinism, the United States would be the last of the major developed countries to move toward the welfare state.

The Birth of the Welfare State

THE modern welfare state was born in Europe, not the United States. Its roots went deep into the past, but they were nourished by the hard realities of nineteenth century industrial society. Many of those realities were similar to conditions in the United States, but there were some key differences as well.

One of the most important of those differences was a European tradition of official involvement in charity, which was very different from the developing tradition in America. During the Middle Ages, the Roman Catholic Church was a virtual partner of many European governments. Many Catholic orders carried out charitable works among the poor that were regarded as at least semigovernmental.[1]

The Poor Laws

When England broke with the Roman Catholic Church in the late sixteenth century, the government took over some of the Church's charitable responsibilities. In 1601, the British government passed the first Poor Law to provide relief to some of the most impoverished people in Britain.[2] Other European countries soon passed similar laws.

The Poor Laws were not entirely charitable, in the usual sense of that word. The Poor Laws were used not just to help the victims of poverty, but to control them. They had as much to do with law enforcement as with charity. One of their main purposes was to cut down the numbers of beggars and thieves who swarmed over England's cities and roamed through its countryside. As one study of the origins of the welfare state puts it, "they were much more reliant on punishments than on relief."[3]

Orphans, for example, were forced into apprenticeship programs, and able-bodied paupers were made to take jobs. By the early eighteenth century, England was establishing poorhouses to house—and to confine—those who were too weak, sick, or incompetent to work.

The English Poor Laws applied throughout England, but it was left to the town governments to administer them. Even the most generous towns kept benefits low. In an age when most workers received barely enough to keep them alive, relief for the poor was held below even the lowest wage.

There were at least two reasons for the towns' stinginess. One was a matter of public policy; there was a widespread belief that the unemployed were lazy, and there was no wish to encourage them in a life of idleness. The other was economic—the taxes that funded the programs were collected locally. The more relief a town provided, the more money it would have to raise to pay for it.

Despite their serious limitations, the Poor Laws did establish the principle that the government had an obligation to help the poorest of the poor. To that extent, they formed a basis for the development of the welfare state.

Industrialization

The Industrial Revolution began even earlier in Europe than in the United States. In Europe, industrialization was a flood that lifted masses of people off the land they had lived on for centuries and swept them into factories in the filthy, crowded cities.

In the great smoky metropolises of Paris, London, and

Berlin, people who had once known generations of their neighbors now lived among strangers. People who had once cooperated with each other to till the land now elbowed each other for space on the teeming city streets.

As peasant farmers, their ancestors had lived in poverty, but at least they'd been sure of a place to live, and land to grow their food. True, the land belonged to the lord of the manor, not to them. But the lord had always had firm obligations toward them. As long as they worked the land for him, he was obliged to provide them a home and a portion of the food they grew. Now, no one was obliged to provide them anything at all.

Just as in America, the daily existence of most industrial workers was hard and unrewarding. They were forever teetering on the edge of poverty. Their greatest fears were of being maimed on the job or falling victim to a serious disease. Both occurrences were common, due to the unhealthy and unsafe working conditions of the time. And if either happened, the worker was almost certain to lose his job. Without insurance, or the money to pay a doctor, he might never be healthy enough to work again. With no money coming in, the worker's family would be thrown out of the hovel they lived in, and into the streets.

Even those lucky enough to escape early accident or disease had nothing to look forward to. They were bound to lose their jobs, sooner or later, to old age and younger workers. When they did, there would be no pension. Since they'd never earned enough to save, they would live out their lives in grinding poverty.

Worst of all, there was no way for most European workers to improve their lot, so their children faced the same miserable fate as they did themselves. There seemed to be no way out of this new working class. By the mid-nineteenth century, there was a growing spirit of restlessness among the workers—and a growing anger.

As Harry Girvetz explains in an article for the *International Encyclopedia of the Social Sciences*: "Unlike earlier societies in which distress was brought about by crop failures and other unavoidable disasters . . . distress was now caused by institutional arrangements"[4]—the institutional arrangements of nineteenth-century capitalism.

Unlike their ancestors, the factory workers had someone—or something—to blame. It was no longer nature or the will of God that was responsible for their poverty and suffering. It was the new social and economic system. And since changes in the system had caused the problem, some of them began to ask, why not change the system to solve it?

Socialism

While the workers grew more and more restless, radical economists and social philosophers were searching for ways to reform the system. Some of them, known as socialists, concluded that the system shouldn't just be changed, it should be destroyed.

Capitalism, they believed, was essentially evil. Why should the wealth generated by industrialization go to the small class of capitalists, while the masses of workers who actually produced that wealth lived in poverty? Instead of individuals owning factories and other economic institutions, they argued, everyone should own them together. Instead of enriching a few capitalists, the wealth the factories produced should be shared more or less equally among the workers.

If capitalism created the conditions for the development of the welfare state, socialism was the spur. Its leading champion was a German scholar named Karl Marx. Marx predicted that the workers would eventually revolt, overthrow the capitalists and install a socialist system that would treat the masses of the people more fairly. He and a fellow reformer named Friedrich Engels called for the workers of the world to unite and throw off their "chains" in a pamphlet called *The Communist Manifesto.*

Many European workers responded to their call. Together with idealistic intellectuals they founded socialist movements all over Europe. Some began referring to themselves as Communists.

These workers' movements were greeted with alarm by the European governments, which were firmly allied with the capitalists in their countries. They saw worker unrest as a threat to the social order, and ultimately to the governments themselves. There was a growing fear that the workers might actually rebel and launch a communist revolution.

Clearly, something had to be done to undermine the socialists, and to head off the threat created by the workers' unrest. Some governments responded with repression and even violence. But, at the same time, some far-thinking leaders were searching desperately for some more permanent way to quiet the workers. It was out of this search that the first modern welfare state was born.

Bismarck's Gamble

German workers were among the most unhappy in Europe. By the late nineteenth century, they were flocking to the socialist Social Democratic Party in droves. Like many other European leaders, the German chancellor, Otto von Bismarck, took strong action against the socialists. His government banned their literature, and he encouraged the police to disrupt their meetings. While these measures temporarily cowed Socialist political activity, they did nothing to cool the bubbling cauldron of the workers' discontent.

But Bismarck was smart enough to realize that force alone could not keep the lid on the cauldron forever. Beginning in 1881, he moved to lower the social tensions by removing some of the underlying worries that fueled the workers' rage. He launched a series of measures that provided German workers with health and accident insurance, as well as pensions to support them when they got too old to work. This ambitious new scheme was paid for jointly by the government, the capitalist employers, and the workers themselves.

By the beginning of the twentieth century, the insurance and pension plans were in place. They gave German workers a security no workers in the western world had had since the Industrial Revolution began.

Bismarck was not particularly sympathetic to the workers, nor was he acting out of concern for their well-being. He was a statesman, acting out of a desire to head off rebellion and a determination to make Germany the leading nation in Europe. To accomplish all that, he needed a stable society and a productive workforce, both of which were threatened by the workers' resentments.

Bismarck reasoned that if anger and insecurity made German workers a threat to his plans, contentment might make them a tool. By providing for the workers' futures, he hoped to make them docile and cooperative. A worker with a pension, Bismarck said, "is much more contented and easier to manage than a man who has no such prospect."[5] It was a gamble, but a gamble worth taking.

It turned out to be a very expensive gamble. From 1880 to 1910, the percentage of the German budget spent on social programs nearly doubled, from about 32 percent to roughly 60 percent. But Bismarck's gamble paid off.

By 1910, Germany was the leading power in western Europe. Its workforce was the envy of its neighbors. What's more, even though it spent most of its budget on social programs, its army was second to none. One reason was the fact that German soldiers, most of whom came from the working class, were in better physical condition than any others in Europe, thanks largely to Bismarck's welfare measures.[6]

Other European Welfare States
With Germany's example before them, virtually all the other western European governments began introducing similar measures.[7] The first to be introduced in many

countries were insurance plans to protect workers against the economic disaster of being injured on the job. These plans were commonly called "workman's compensation insurance." (It was assumed that most industrial workers would be male.) By the turn of the century, most western European countries had compensation plans; by 1911 all of them did.

By that time, most western European countries had also introduced other forms of social insurance, all subsidized (or partly paid for) by the government. Some plans were voluntary, and only covered people who chose to pay into the plan. Others were compulsory. In general, the compulsory plans were more effective because they covered a broader section of the population.

Eight countries had some form of old-age insurance, or government-assisted pension plans, to provide for workers when they were too old to work. At least nine had introduced some form of government-assisted sickness insurance. Although these were designed to cover non-work-related health problems, they were usually limited to workers. There was no coverage for other family members, or for the unemployed.

In fact, aid of any kind for the unemployed was slow in coming. There was still a deep feeling that people who didn't have a job must be lazy, or "undeserving" in some other way. Even when unemployment insurance plans began to be introduced, most were voluntary. Only Germany, Austria, Italy, and the United Kingdom required employers to enroll in the plans from the time they were introduced.

Britain was relatively slow to start on the road to the welfare state, but once it began, it moved quickly. A far-reaching national old-age pension plan was adopted in 1908, and a partial minimum wage was in place by 1909. In 1911, Prime Minister Lloyd George introduced a national unemployment and health insurance plan that was one of the most progressive in the world.

Many of the early social insurance plans were extremely limited, in both the range of people they covered and the amount of benefits they provided. But they represented a historic commitment on the part of the governments involved. They meant that the governments were accepting at least some of the responsibility for the economic well-being of their citizens.

Why the Welfare State Developed

Why did so many governments choose that time to make that historic commitment? To some extent, they were attempting to pacify the growing anger of the working class. But there were other reasons as well.

One important factor was the economic success of industrialization itself. The productivity and efficiency made possible by the new machines generated enormous profits. There was more than enough wealth to go around. That wealth made it possible to provide new benefits to masses of the people.

But the mere fact that great wealth existed did not necessarily mean that it would be shared. There were at least two social and political factors at work in the nineteenth century that pushed Europe in the direction of the welfare state. The first was the spread of democracy. Throughout the western world, people had been demanding—and getting—a greater voice in their governments. Now they were using that voice to call for measures that would benefit them. To some extent, the social insurance plans adopted by the western governments were ways of answering that call. In a sense, the welfare state can be thought of as a kind of economic democracy.

But democracy was not the only great social idea on the rise in the nineteenth century. There was also a growing spirit of altruism—a sense that the welfare of others was the duty of everyone. Meanwhile, the old idea that economic misfortune must be a sign of moral guilt was breaking down. The raw unfairness of nineteenth-century capitalism was glaringly obvious to almost everyone. Writers as different as Karl Marx and the British novelist Charles Dickens called the abuses and cruelties suffered by the urban poor to public attention. It was not just the workers who were demanding that something be done about the suffering of the poor. Altruistic intellectuals, scholars, social activists, and members of the middle class were demanding it as well.

All of these factors—economic, social and philosophic—combined to generate the modern welfare state. By the time World War I broke out in 1914, every government in western Europe had accepted its responsibility to provide some kind of safety net for its people. Of all the western democracies, only the United States remained uncommitted to this fundamental principle of the welfare state.

The Development of the American Welfare State

NOT until the Great Depression of the 1930s did the United States finally begin to install programs similar to those Europe had had for decades.

The Great Depression

The Great Depression was the worst economic disaster the developed world had seen since the Industrial Revolution began. For the United States, it began with the stock market crash in October 1929.

Thousands of investors had borrowed money to buy stocks during the 1920s, when stock prices seemed sure to keep going up forever. When prices plummeted, many of them lost everything they had. Some lost *more* than they had. Stuck with almost worthless stocks, they still had to pay for the money they'd borrowed. Cartoons of the time pictured investors in top hats and tuxedos leaping from the windows of investment houses. It really wasn't funny. Some bankrupt investors did just that.

Investors who rushed to sell their assets often found they couldn't raise enough to pay back their loans. The unpaid loans were like dominoes. Before long the banks that had made the bad loans started going under. They called in their mortgage loans. People who couldn't afford to pay off the mortgages on their homes found themselves in the streets. People who couldn't pay off the mortgages on their farms or businesses had to sell them, or close them down. Despite a desperate calling in of loans, 5,000 banks failed within a few years,[1] taking with them the savings of millions of depositors.

Every failed business and farm meant people out of work—not just the owner, but everyone who'd worked there. The number of unemployed Americans doubled in the first year of the Great Depression, to roughly 3 million. The next year, it more than doubled again. By the end of 1932, there would be roughly 12 million Americans out of work.[2]

Since there was no unemployment insurance, many of the 12 million were thrown into sudden poverty, and their spouses and children along with them.

The jobless and the homeless were everywhere. Armies of them roamed the highways, wandering the country in search of work. They slept under bridges, grabbing what shelter they could from the wind and rain. They clustered together in temporary huts slapped together from scraps of wood and tar paper on vacant city lots. They called the makeshift villages "Hoovervilles," after Republican President Herbert Hoover, who seemed either unwilling or unable to do anything to help them.

President Hoover sympathized, but insisted the downturn was only temporary. "The fundamental business of the country," he insisted, "is on a sound and prosperous basis."[3] In the meantime, he tried to convince businesses to create more jobs, and called on all employed Americans to contribute to the Red Cross and other private charities that gave help to the unemployed.

Like many government leaders before him, Hoover was convinced that it would be wrong for the federal government to give direct help to the poor. That, he insisted, "would impair something infinitely valuable in the life of the American people."[4]

Without leadership from the federal government,

some states began to act on their own. New York became
the first to set up an emergency relief agency in 1931.
Wisconsin became the first to establish a government-run
unemployment insurance program in 1932. But the states'
efforts were too small to deal with the multiplying masses
of people thrown into poverty by unemployment.

Stubbornly refusing to give direct aid to the unemployed, Hoover did what the U.S. government had always
done when the country's economic welfare needed pro-
moting—he gave more help to business. He set up the
Reconstruction Finance Corporation to loan $2 billion to
the railroads, banks, and other major industries. He also
made $300 million in loans available to farmers, and gave
the construction industry a boost with a massive federal
program to build new highways, public buildings, and
airports.[5] All of this government spending resulted in
thousands of new jobs, but there were *millions* of unemployed workers.

As in Europe fifty years earlier, some restless workers
turned to socialism, and to radical unions like the Wob-
blies (the Industrial Workers of the World). And, again as
in Europe, some wealthy people began to fear a revolution,
and some American workers began dreaming of it.

The New Deal

In the presidential campaign of 1932, the Democratic presidential candidate, Franklin D. Roosevelt, pledged the
American people "a new deal" if he were elected. He did
not spell out what this new deal would consist of, but he
didn't have to. The willingness to do almost anything new
appealed to a public that was angry with Hoover's inability
to end the Depression. Voters not only elected Roosevelt,
they elected a majority Democratic Congress to serve with
him.

President Roosevelt acted quickly to show people the
new administration was ready, willing, and able to act.
Two days after his inauguration, he dramatically closed

the country's banks. During the "bank holiday" that followed, he called for a special session of Congress to pass measures to combat the Depression. When the banks reopened a few days later, he assured the public it was now safe to keep their money in them. Most people believed him. It wasn't so much *what* the president had done to help the banks, but the fact that he had done *something*. For the first time since the Depression began, there was a sense that the federal government was ready to do what was needed to make things better.

Economic Rights

No one really knew what was needed to end the Depression, or even what would really help. But the same uncertainty that had made Hoover cautious made Roosevelt bold. Hoover had been anxious not to do anything that might make things worse. Roosevelt was determined to try anything that might make things better.

The first three months of his administration, a period which became known as the Hundred Days, was a whirlwind of activity. Major new agencies sprang up overnight—to help farmers and homeowners meet their mortgages, to regulate the stock market (whose crash had started the disaster in the first place), to promote fair competition in business. After that, the rush of new programs slowed down a bit, but it wouldn't come to a stop for at least five years.

It was soon clear that the New Deal was more than a political slogan. It was a reality that would change the nature of the American government, and of its relationship to the well-being of its people.

Roosevelt proposed what amounted to a new Bill of Rights. The original Bill of Rights established Americans' basic political rights. This one would establish Americans' economic rights, including the right to work at a job that paid a living wage and the rights to comfortable housing, good education, and medical care.[6] No actual bill of economic rights was ever enacted, but much of the New Deal seemed to assume that these things were, in fact, the birthright of every American.

The New Deal took a scattershot approach to solving the problems of the Great Depression.[7] Measures designed to provide relief to the poor, reform to the financial system, and recovery to American business were all mixed up together.

Many New Deal programs simply extended what Hoover had already done. The Reconstruction Finance Corporation was enlarged, for example, and more money was authorized for government building projects. These projects not only provided jobs, they boosted the economy by putting billions of dollars of federal spending into circulation.

But much of the New Deal was really new. Several new programs were designed to help workers, both employed and unemployed. The Federal Emergency Relief Administration provided direct federal grants (not just loans) to the states for the purpose of giving immediate food and other help to the poor. In time, this emergency relief was largely replaced by job relief: a complex of programs designed to give work—and incomes—to millions of the unemployed.

Direct relief programs were loudly attacked by conservatives who had supported Hoover. Providing help to the unemployed, they argued, only undermined their ambition to get a job. Besides, they argued, help for the unemployed drained money from businesses and working taxpayers. The money had to come from somewhere. Some of this opposition revealed the old prejudice against the poor, the idea that somehow the unfortunate deserved their lot. Many conservatives simply felt that it was unfair to increase the tax burden on working people to help those who were too lazy, or too incompetent, to work themselves. The federal government was taking on too much, they complained, and would only make things worse in the long run. But, "People don't eat 'in the long run,' " a New Dealer named Harry Hopkins retorted. "They eat everyday."[8]

The New Deal initiated a variety of measures that helped workers to help themselves. Among them was the National Labor Relations Act, which protected their right to organize into unions. Other major innovations came in the Fair Labor Standards Act of 1938, which set a national minimum wage and limited the number of hours many employers could force workers to work in a given week.

A special effort was made to help the young. The National Youth Administration gave part-time jobs to unemployed young people between sixteen and twenty-five, and provided many of them support to go to high school or college. One of the most unusual jobs programs was the Emergency Conservation Work agency, or Civilian Conservation Corp (CCC). The CCC employed young men between the ages of seventeen and twenty-three in a variety of projects designed to beautify or preserve the environment. The men, who had to be both single and unemployed to join, were paid very little, but they got free room and board in military-style work camps. Over the nearly ten years it existed, the CCC kept almost 3 million young workers reasonably healthy and out of the "hobo jungles," at least for awhile.

Several New Deal programs were specially designed to improve the quality of life for those rural Americans who had been left behind in the great migration to the cities. The Tennessee Valley Authority (TVA) launched a massive federal experiment to develop the Tennessee River Valley region of the southeastern United States. The Rural Electrification Administration (REA) brought the benefit of electricity to millions of rural Americans who would never have gotten it otherwise. This may seem like a small thing, until you consider that it was only the coming of electricity that allowed isolated rural people to have refrigerators, electric lights, washing machines, and even radios. The

REA brought millions of these rural Americans into the twentieth century.[9]

The Social Security Act

Most New Deal relief programs were meant to be temporary—stop-gap responses to the economic emergency of the Great Depression. They were intended to last only as long as the emergency lasted. Most of them, in fact, were abolished in the 1940s. One great exception, however, was the social insurance system established by a series of acts starting in 1935.

The original Social Security system consisted of measures designed to give some financial protection, or security, to the elderly, and to workers and their families. These measures were mandated (or required) by the federal government, but they were administered by the states. They were paid for by forced contributions from both workers and their employers.

The heart of Social Security was a national system of old-age pensions for retired workers. Every time a worker received a paycheck, part of her or his wages would be deducted and paid into the system. At the same time, the employer would be required to make an equal payment on the worker's behalf. When workers retired, they would receive small monthly payments from the program, which would last until death.

To help those already too old to work, the Social Security Act of 1935 also provided for payments to the elderly poor, to be funded partly by the states and partly by the federal government. The maximum payment was $30 a month, with half coming from the federal government and half from the state.

Other early Social Security benefits went to the blind, the physically disabled, crippled children, and mothers with children who had no way to support themselves.

Although many women worked outside the home even then, it was considered vital that a mother be at home to raise the children. It was still assumed that the "normal" family would have a working father and a home-making mother. But when a husband and father died or deserted a family, the wife and children were left without support. Widows' pensions and help for half-orphaned children had long been a concern of social activists. Now, at least some federal help was made available to some husbandless mothers and dependent children. This help eventually developed into the current Aid to Families with Dependent Children program that most people think of as "welfare" today.

Only the most conservative opponents of the New Deal would argue with the need to help the elderly poor and crippled children. But another provision of the Social Security Act was much more controversial. That was unemployment insurance. Even with millions of people unemployed, there was still a certain prejudice against those who were not working. Knowing there would be a great outcry against any direct, long-term federal help for the unemployed, Congress directed the states to set up their own unemployment insurance systems.

Most states already required employers to provide some form of workmen's compensation insurance for injured workers. Although established by state law, these programs were funded by the employers. Now, the federal government encouraged the states to extend these programs to workers who lost their jobs for other reasons or to set up separate insurance systems for laid-off workers. Any state that did not willingly set up a program that met minimum federal standards would be ordered to do so.

Social Security was similar to the social insurance programs in Europe, but it didn't go nearly as far as most of them. It did not apply to all workers, its benefits were small, and they varied from state to state. But, unlike most other New Deal programs, it was a long-term program, intended to be in effect long after the New Deal itself. More than any other single New Deal measure, it represented a permanent commitment to the welfare state.

The Heritage of the New Deal

Some New Deal measures, like the REA, were obvious successes. Others were obvious failures. As the twentieth century draws to a close, economists still debate whether the New Deal saved the economy from total collapse or lengthened the Great Depression and deepened its effects.

But whatever else it did, the New Deal set the United States on a no-exit highway to the modern welfare state. It established a definite federal role in providing relief to the poor and jobs to the unemployed. Having once taken on that role, the government would not be able to give it up. The Great Depression had revealed to Americans the potential for disaster that lay beneath their free enterprise economy. It made them chillingly aware that they lived on the edge of personal financial catastrophe. Having once supplied them with a safety net to catch them if they fell, the government could hardly just take it away and leave them unprotected again.

The Fair Deal

Harry S Truman, the Democratic president who followed Roosevelt, tried to build on what the New Deal had begun. He proposed constructing massive new public works projects, raising the minimum wage, enlarging Social Security, and strengthening federal regulation of the way businesses treated workers. But Truman's plans, which he called the Fair Deal, went beyond expanding current programs. He also proposed ambitious new measures, including a large-scale federal program of slum clearance and construction of low-income housing, federal aid to education, and—most radical of all—an extensive national health insurance program.[10]

Except for national health insurance and federal aid

to education, the bulk of the Fair Deal eventually became law. But as the historians Allan Nevins and Henry Steele Commager point out, "the most important immediate result of the Fair Deal program was that it protected the New Deal gains already won."[11]

Even after the Republicans took over in 1952, they made no serious effort to dismantle the social welfare system. In fact, under the Republican President Dwight D. Eisenhower, both the Social Security and unemployment compensation programs were extended to cover millions more people. In 1950, two years before Eisenhower took office, roughly 8 million people got some form of government social assistance. By the time he left office ten years later, the number had soared to 20 million.[12] It was also under Eisenhower that the federal government's commitment to the public welfare was emphasized by the creation of the Department of Health, Education, and Welfare in 1953. Although conservative Republicans opposed many welfare programs, the basic reality of the welfare state had clearly been accepted by the mainstreams of both major political parties.

The War on Poverty
Next to Franklin Roosevelt, no president did more to establish the American welfare state than Lyndon B. Johnson. The economy was beginning to boom when Johnson took office in 1963. An old New Dealer, he proclaimed his desire to build a "Great Society," which would use America's enormous wealth "to enrich and elevate our national life—and to advance the quality of American civilization."[13]

But Johnson believed a Great Society had to be a fair society. Even in the midst of the economic boom, almost 40 million Americans were living in poverty.[14] A great many of them were black. Segregation was still legally enforced in much of the country, and many African Americans were becoming restless and angry under the twin weights of poverty and racial discrimination.

In 1964, Johnson declared a massive "war on poverty." To fight it, he established a new agency called the Office of Economic Opportunity (OEO). Its job was to oversee the largest array of new social welfare programs since the New Deal.

Many OEO programs tried to prepare poor people to help themselves. These included the Job Corps, which trained impoverished young people in the skills they needed to get and hold a job, and a variety of Community Action Programs, designed to show poor people how to organize to create political, economic, and social change.

A great emphasis was put on education at all levels. The Head Start Program was launched to prepare poor and otherwise disadvantaged children to enter grade school. Large-scale federal aid to education was established for the first time. And the College Work Study Program was put in place to help poor and middle class young people work their way through college.

More than anything since the New Deal, it was the Great Society/War on Poverty that constructed the American welfare state. It made millions more people eligible for existing programs, swelling the government assistance rolls and increasing the benefits of existing programs such as Aid to Dependent Children and food stamps.

But perhaps the most important of all the Great Society programs were two that dealt with the controversial area of government-supported health care. Health care costs in the United States were already rising dramatically at that time. Fewer and fewer people could afford to pay the medical bills from a serious illness themselves. But the possible enormous costs and the fear of "socialized medicine" had always been enough to block any effort to launch a national health insurance system.

In 1965 President Johnson managed to push two major

health insurance programs through Congress. One, called Medicare, helped people over sixty-five to meet their medical costs. The other, known as Medicaid, helped to pay the medical bills of poor Americans who were too young to qualify for Medicare.

In signing the Medicare bill, Johnson paid tribute to the president who had first proposed government-sponsored health insurance. He held the signing ceremony in the Harry S Truman Library in Truman's hometown, with the aging ex-president sitting by his side.[15]

Neither Medicare nor Medicaid was as far-reaching as the government medical programs in Europe, but they still cost a huge amount of money. In Medicaid's first year, for example, it cost the federal government ten times more than its supporters had predicted. The program's rules were quickly changed to lower the number of people eligible.[16]

Backlash

Even while waging the war on poverty, the country was waging a war in Vietnam. The growing costs of both put an enormous strain on the economic boom that had marked the early and middle 1960s. This led to a backlash against the growth of the welfare state, among both politicians and taxpayers alike. As a result, Johnson's successor, Richard Nixon, led the first real attempt to shrink the welfare state.

Nixon favored reducing the federal role in social welfare. He wanted some welfare measures drastically reduced or eliminated, and more responsibility for the others to be shifted to state and local governments. Even Nixon, however, did not strike at Social Security or the other New Deal programs that were at the heart of the welfare state. Instead, he hacked away at some newer Great Society programs, while firmly vetoing new federal welfare measures passed by the Democratic Congress.

At the time he was forced from office by the Watergate

scandal, he was planning to end federal support to more than a hundred social welfare programs and projects around the country. In 1973, his last year as president, he dealt the war on poverty a parting blow by dismantling the Office of Economic Opportunity.

Despite Nixon's efforts, the costs of social welfare programs kept increasing. By 1980, when Ronald Reagan won election to the presidency, federal spending on all social programs had climbed to $244 billion.[17] More than half the total was accounted for by Social Security.

Reagan came into office promising to lower taxes and eliminate the federal budget deficit. In order to cut federal spending, he launched the fiercest assault yet on the welfare state. Attacking across a broad front, he slashed spending for programs like food stamps and job training, changed the rules to make fewer people eligible, and even proposed cuts in Social Security.

But even Reagan didn't try to get rid of the welfare state entirely. Instead, he tried to shrink the welfare system and drastically reduce government spending on social programs of all kinds. Aided by a cooperative Congress, he proceeded to eliminate some programs, tighten the rules to squeeze as many people as possible out of the rest, and reduce benefits for many who remained. New federal rules also made it easier for states to cut their own welfare rolls, dropping large numbers of people from joint state-federal programs. Many states proceeded to do just that in attempts to cut their own welfare budgets.

Reagan's effort to shrink the welfare system was not a great success. Federal social spending was clearly lower under Reagan than it would have been without him; and hundreds of thousands, if not millions, of people were dropped from state welfare rolls. But, overall, welfare spending actually continued to grow even during Reagan's presidency.

The main reason was a tremendous growth in the number of poor people. According to government figures, the poverty rate climbed by a third, and the number of poor people rose from just over 26 million in 1979 to 35½ million in 1983.[18] Although both the rate and the number then started to drop a little, there were still roughly 6 million more poor people in the United States when Reagan left office in 1988 than when he entered it. And even that figure may underestimate the change, since the government revised its definition of poverty during that time.

Critics of the Reagan administration blamed the worsening poverty on the recent changes in welfare policies. Columnist Christopher Matthews argues that over 40 percent of the increase that took place in the 1980s was due to "reduction in government benefit programs at the federal, state, and local levels."[19] Those reductions are still having an effect today.

The reductions involved more than benefit cuts. Some of the most dramatic cuts came in low-income housing. From 1981 to 1988, the Reagan administration slashed support for low-income housing from $32 billion to $7.5 billion. The result was a net loss in the number of affordable apartments and houses available for the poor. During the few years before Reagan took office, 500,000 new low-income units had been built, but during his two terms only 25,000 were added. At the same time, 500,000 low-income housing units were being abandoned, destroyed, or replaced by higher-priced condominiums, each year.[20] The number of homeless people rose dramatically.

Reagan won many battles in his war on the welfare state, but not the war itself. Reagan's assault on welfare spending left the basic structure of the welfare state intact. The idea of cutting welfare was very popular. The idea of eliminating it was not. Just cutting overall welfare spending proved impossible. Even while Reagan-era rule changes were forcing many people off welfare, poverty caused by those same changes was forcing others on. Even while individual benefits were being cut, total government spending on benefits was increasing.

It seems that however angry Americans get about the size and expense of the welfare state, they remain committed to the idea of welfare. No one, or almost no one, wants to stand by while their fellow Americans suffer. Even Reagan himself always talked about the need for a "safety net" to protect what he called the "truly needy."

The year after Reagan left office, the head of a Ford Foundation study of the welfare system could still report that "our social welfare system has remained sturdy over the years."[21] That system has never been perfect. The safety net never prevented everyone from falling into poverty. And the Reagan assault left it even weaker and less reliable than it used to be. But, as we will see in the next two chapters, it is still very much in place.

Social Security: Foundation of the Welfare State

IN the next two chapters, we will examine some of the biggest and most visible of United States public assistance programs. But readers should not make the mistake of assuming that the American welfare state is made up entirely of programs like these.

The modern welfare state involves much more than services to the poor or to people who face unexpected financial problems. The modern welfare state rests on a broad foundation of government policies, programs, agencies, regulations, subsidies, and laws—most of which people never think of as welfare at all.

As Floyd Hyde, a former assistant secretary of the Department of Housing and Urban Development, has pointed out:

> *Americans who pride themselves as rugged individualists go through life attending public schools, receiving veterans' benefits, financing homes with FHA mortgages, retiring on Social Security, or even receiving payments for not growing certain crops. But all these were regarded as public rights and [as] somehow different from welfare payments which are regarded as handouts to the ungrateful poor . . . and if to the list we add . . . [those people who] use Medicare, complete*

GI Bill financed education or receive investment credits on their taxes, or even work for companies with large government contracts, then we have few people who are not on welfare."[1]

"It Isn't Welfare, Is It?"

All of the government programs mentioned above, along with hundreds of others, benefit middle- and upper-class Americans at least as much as they help the poor. Some benefit *only* members of the middle or upper class. Yet they are all important building blocks of the welfare state. One of them, Social Security, is the biggest of all government social programs. It pays more benefits to more people than any other federal program of any kind. And yet, if asked, most recipients and politicians alike would deny that Social Security is a welfare program.

The effort to divorce Social Security from welfare began when the program was first launched in 1935. "Now, this is a *pension* program. It isn't *welfare*, is it?" President Roosevelt asked nervously, before signing the Social Security bill into law.[2]

The effort to erect a wall between Social Security and welfare continues to this day. It has been extremely effective. Most Americans do not think of Social Security as welfare. Almost everyone eligible to receive Social Security benefits accepts them happily. Yet, some of the same people refuse even to apply for other government benefits. They are too proud, they insist, to take welfare.

Why should there be this separation? Social Security, after all, is a social insurance program, the same kind of program that first earned Germany and other European countries the description of welfare states. Why are so many Americans determined not to think of Social Security as welfare? Why are so many politicians reluctant even to discuss Social Security and welfare in the same conversation?

There are two main reasons. The less important of the two is a technical one. In theory, Social Security is different because it is a self-paid insurance program. It is not, according to this same theory, even a part of the federal budget. Its benefits are not paid from the federal treasury, but from special trust funds collected by a specific tax on the earnings of individuals.

There is some merit to this technical distinction, although less than there used to be. The government has recently started subtracting the amount in the Social Security trust funds from the federal debt. In one sense, this includes Social Security in the budget, and weakens the distinction between it and other social programs.

What is more, benefits are paid whether there is enough money in the trust funds to cover them or not. In the late 1970s and early 1980s, there was less money than needed in the trust funds, by 1991 there was considerably more. But it hardly seemed to matter. The government has always paid the benefits owed, and insists that it always will, regardless of what is in the trust funds.

But the main reason Social Security is not classified as a welfare program is political. There has always been a stigma attached to the idea of welfare. People do not like to think of themselves as being on welfare. And yet, almost every American is enrolled in the Social Security system. Babies often get Social Security numbers soon after birth. Roughly one out of every six Americans actually received some form of Social Security benefit in 1990, and eventually almost everyone who lives to retirement age will probably receive Social Security benefits. No one likes to think of everyone in America as being on welfare.

The distinction between welfare and Social Security implies certain things about welfare. For one thing, it implies that welfare is meant to be an emergency measure, designed to help people survive temporary financial setbacks. Except for such emergencies, it implies, welfare is to be reserved for the unhappy exceptions in society—the seriously disabled and the mentally incompetent. It is certainly not something that applies to ordinary Americans. Most of all, it implies that welfare is a form of charity. It is *given*. Social Security, on the other hand, is *earned*.

But these distinctions are not as clear as they may seem. It is true that most Social Security recipients (or their parents or spouses) have paid taxes into the Social Security system. In that sense, they have earned the benefits they receive. But most recipients of other welfare benefits have also paid many taxes in their lives. Even the people currently "on welfare" pay sales taxes, and sometimes other taxes as well.

Whether Social Security is considered a part of the *welfare system* or not, it is a fundamental part of the *welfare state*—that is, the whole structure of programs that establishes government's role in providing for the basic economic needs of the people. And it is the fact that Social Security covers virtually everyone that makes it so fundamental to this structure.

Social Security takes the government's commitment to the idea of social welfare beyond the limits of the safety net. It provides support in good times and bad. What's more, it provides support to everyone enrolled in the system, not just those who have suffered unexpected economic disaster. This is what makes Social Security more than just another welfare program. It is, in reality, the foundation on which the American welfare state is built.

Retirement, Disability, and Death Benefits

"The basic idea behind Social Security is a simple one," a government booklet explains. "You pay taxes into the system during your working years, and you and members of your family receive monthly benefits when you retire or become disabled. Or, your survivors collect benefits when you die."[3]

Today's massive Social Security system is administered by the federal Social Security Administration, a division of the Department of Health and Human Services. The trust funds that support it are supplied by a tax on most workers' earnings, up to a certain level. In 1990, the amount of earnings subject to the tax was $51,300; in 1991, it rose to $53,400. Most employees who work for wages never see the money at all. Employers automatically deduct, or withhold, a certain percentage from each worker's paycheck before the worker even receives it. In 1991, the percentage was 7.65. In addition, the employer is required to pay another 7.65 percent itself. In theory, then, each (the worker and the employer) pays half the tax. Self-employed workers have to pay the whole 15.3 percent themselves.

In general, a worker has to pay into the system for about ten years before he or she becomes fully vested; that is, before becoming eligible for full benefits. (Young workers become eligible for disability benefits a little sooner.) Once workers are vested, they are entitled to receive benefits when they retire or become disabled. Once they reach age sixty-five, they are also eligible for Medicare, the federal program that pays for medical care for the elderly. If a worker dies leaving a dependent spouse or child, benefits are paid to the survivors.

The specific amount of benefits any particular person receives depends on how much he or she made, on average, over the bulk of their working life. For most people, the monthly benefit is about 42 percent of their average monthly income. The percentage is lower for people with higher average paychecks, and higher for those with relatively small incomes. This, the Social Security Administration explains, is "because the . . . benefit formula is weighted in favor of low income workers who have less opportunity to save and invest during their working years."[4]

Medicare

Social Security provides certain other important benefits besides disability, retirement, and death insurance. The most important of these is Medicare.

Medicare has two main programs, or "parts." Part A covers hospital bills and follow-up care, while Part B covers doctors' fees and other medical expenses not covered by Part A. All Social Security recipients are automatically enrolled in Part A (hospital insurance) as soon as they reach age sixty-five, or have been receiving Social Security disability payments for at least a year. In addition, spouses and certain other family members of people eligible for Medicare may also be eligible. So are people receiving railroad retirement benefits, as well as some people with permanent kidney failure.

In general, Part A helps pay for inpatient care in hospitals, skilled nursing facilities, and hospices as well as caregiving visits by Medicare-approved health professionals to patients confined to their homes.

Anyone eligible for Part A is also eligible for Part B (medical insurance). But, unlike Part A, Part B is optional, and comes at a price. Anyone wishing to enroll in Part B has to pay a monthly premium of $29.90 a month. People who don't sign up for Part B during the first seven months they are eligible pay a penalty if they join late. They can then only sign up during the first three months of later years, and when they do, their monthly premium will be 10 percent higher for each year they were eligible to belong but didn't. This is to prevent people from waiting until they are sick to enroll.

Part B helps pay doctor's bills; outpatient care visits to hospitals, laboratory and X-ray tests done specifically to diagnose disease, as well as needed ambulance rides and certain other kinds of medical services and supplies.

Medicare is far from a total health insurance program. It does not cover certain health-related expenses at all. These include regular physical examinations; dental care; eye exams; and expenses relating to dentures, eyeglasses, or hearing aids. Most significantly, for the elderly people who benefit from Medicare, it does not cover either prescription drugs or routine nursing home expenses, both of which can be extremely expensive.

Even covered expenses, like inpatient hospital care, are not paid completely. In 1991, for example, the first sixty days of an extended hospital stay was covered, but patients still had to pay $628 of the total bill themselves. If they had to be in the hospital longer than sixty days, they had to pay $157 a day up to ninety days. After that, Medicare patients were totally uncovered, unless they chose to use some of the sixty so-called "reserve days" Medicare allows them in their whole lifetime. During reserve days, Medicare will continue to pay hospital expenses over and above the first $314 a day, which still has to be paid by the patient.[5]

Part B coverage is even more limited. There is a yearly $100 deductible, which means that the patient must pay the first $100 of covered charges. And even after that, Medicare will only pay a percentage of covered expenses. Medicare decides what it considers a reasonable charge for specific medical services, but then it will only pay a percentage of that. Since many doctors charge more than Medicare considers reasonable, patients sometimes have to pay 30 percent, 40 percent, or even more of supposedly covered medical expenses themselves.

Medicare recipients who can afford it often buy private insurance to help pay the portions of their medical bills the program doesn't cover. Local and cable television are filled with commercials for this kind of "Medicare supplement" insurance. According to elderly and consumer groups, these ads are often misleading, and the plans are often overpriced. What's more, many of these supplement policies have big gaps of their own. People sometimes find they have to buy two, or even more, supplementary policies to really cover themselves. Then they find they are paying extra for duplicate coverage of many possible expenses, just to cover the gaps.

Relying on Social Security

The Social Security Administration warns Americans that "Social Security is not intended to be your only source of income. Instead, it is meant to be used to supplement the pensions, insurance, savings, and other investments you will accumulate during your working years."[6]

In theory, then, Social Security is seen as a part of the safety net. Most Americans, the government seems to feel, should be able to provide themselves with a good retirement income without relying on Social Security. Social Security is only there as a cushion, to soften things a little bit, to protect them if their main source of income fails to meet all their needs.

But that is only in theory. In reality, most elderly Americans rely heavily on Social Security—and particularly on Medicare—to meet their basic needs. Many of the elderly, in fact, have no other retirement income at all. They are the ones whose investments went sour, or who never earned enough to make investments or accumulate savings in the first place. They worked at jobs that had no pension plan, or for one of the many companies whose pension plans went bankrupt.

For them, Social Security turns out to be exactly what the Social Security Administration warns it should not be: the only source of income they have once their working lives are over. And their numbers seem likely to increase. Six out of ten retired people today do not receive pensions from their work, and over half of all the Americans working at jobs today have no pension plan.[7] What's more, most of the new jobs that are being

We the People

of the United States, in Order to form a more perfect Union, establish Justice, insure domestic Tranquility, provide for the common Defence, promote the general Welfare, and secure the Blessings of Liberty to ourselves and our Posterity, do ordain and establish this CONSTITUTION for the United States of America.

Article I.

SECTION 1. All legislative Powers herein granted shall be vested in a Congress of the United States, which shall consist of a Senate and House of Representatives.

SECTION 2. The House of Representatives shall be composed of Members chosen every second Year by the People of the several States, and the Electors in each State shall have the Qualifications requisite for Electors of the most numerous Branch of the State Legislature.

No Person shall be a Representative who shall not have attained to the Age of twenty-five Years, and been seven Years a Citizen of the United States, and who shall not, when elected, be an Inhabitant of that State in which he shall be chosen.

[Representatives and direct Taxes shall be apportioned among the several States which may be included within this Union, according to their respective Numbers, which shall be determined by adding to the whole Number of free Persons, including those bound to Service for a Term of Years, and excluding Indians not taxed, three fifths of all other Persons.] The actual Enumeration shall be made within three Years after the first Meeting of the Congress of the United States, and within every subsequent Term of ten Years, in such Manner as they shall by Law direct. The Number of Representatives shall not exceed one for every thirty Thousand, but each State shall have at Least one Representative; and until such enumeration shall be made, the State of New Hampshire shall be entitled to chuse three, Massachusetts eight, Rhode-Island and Providence Plantations one, Connecticut five, New-York six, New Jersey four, Pennsylvania eight, Delaware one, Maryland six, Virginia ten, North Carolina five, South Carolina five, and Georgia three.

When vacancies happen in the Representation from any State, the Executive Authority thereof shall issue Writs of Election to fill such Vacancies.

The House of Representatives shall chuse their Speaker and other Officers; and shall have the sole Power of Impeachment.

SECTION 3. The Senate of the United States shall be composed of two Senators from each State, chosen by the Legislature thereof, for six Years; and each Senator shall have one Vote.

Immediately after they shall be assembled in Consequence of the first Election, they shall be divided as equally as may be into three Classes. The Seats of the Senators of the first Class shall be vacated at the Expiration of the second Year, of the second Class at the Expiration of the fourth Year, and of the third Class at the Expiration of the sixth Year, so that one-third may be chosen every second Year; and if Vacancies happen by Resignation, or otherwise, during the Recess of the Legislature of any State, the Executive thereof may make temporary Appointments until the next Meeting of the Legislature, which shall then fill such Vacancies.

No Person shall be a Senator who shall not have attained to the Age of thirty Years, and been nine Years a Citizen of the United States, and who shall not, when elected, be an Inhabitant of that State for which he shall be chosen.

The Vice President of the United States shall be President of the Senate, but shall have no Vote, unless they be equally divided.

The Senate shall chuse their other Officers, and also a President pro tempore, in the Absence of the Vice President, or when he shall exercise the Office of President of the United States.

The Senate shall have the sole Power to try all Impeachments. When sitting for that Purpose, they shall be on Oath or Affirmation. When the President of the United States is tried, the Chief Justice shall preside: And no Person shall be convicted without the Concurrence of two thirds of the Members present.

Judgment in Cases of Impeachment shall not extend further than to removal from Office, and disqualification to hold and enjoy any Office of honor, Trust or Profit under the United States: but the Party convicted shall nevertheless be liable and subject to Indictment, Trial, Judgment and Punishment, according to Law.

SECTION 4. The Times, Places and Manner of holding Elections for Senators and Representatives, shall be prescribed in each State by the Legislature thereof; but the Congress may at any time by Law make or alter such Regulations, except as to the Place of Chusing Senators.

The Congress shall assemble at least once in every Year, and such Meeting shall be on the first Monday in December, unless they shall by Law appoint a different Day.

SECTION 5. Each House shall be the Judge of the Elections, Returns and Qualifications of its own Members, and a Majority of each shall constitute a Quorum to do Business; but a smaller number may adjourn from day to day, and may be authorized to compel the Attendance of absent Members, in such Manner, and under such Penalties as each House may provide.

Each House may determine the Rules of its Proceedings, punish its Members for disorderly Behavior, and, with the Concurrence of two thirds, expel a Member.

Each House shall keep a Journal of its Proceedings, and from time to time publish the same, excepting such Parts as may in their Judgment require Secrecy; and the Yeas and Nays of the Members of either House on any question shall, at the Desire of one fifth of those Present, be entered on the Journal.

Neither House, during the Session of Congress, shall, without the Consent of the other, adjourn for more than three days, nor to any other Place than that in which the two Houses shall be sitting.

SECTION 6. The Senators and Representatives shall receive a Compensation for their Services, to be ascertained by Law, and paid out of the Treasury of the United States. They shall in all Cases, except Treason, Felony and Breach of the Peace, be privileged from Arrest during their Attendance at the Session of their respective Houses, and in going to and returning from the same; and for any Speech or Debate in either House, they shall not be questioned in any other Place.

No Senator or Representative shall, during the Time for which he was elected, be appointed to any civil Office under the Authority of the United States, which shall have been created, or the Emoluments whereof shall have been encreased during such time; and no Person holding any Office under the United States, shall be a Member of either House during his Continuance in Office.

SECTION 7. All Bills for raising Revenue shall originate in the House of Representatives; but the Senate may propose or concur with Amendments as on other Bills.

Every Bill which shall have passed the House of Representatives and the Senate, shall, before it become a Law, be presented to the President of the United States; If he approve he shall sign it, but if not he shall return it, with his Objections to that House in which it shall have originated, who shall enter the Objections at large on their journal, and proceed to reconsider it. If after such Reconsideration two thirds of that House shall agree to pass the Bill, it shall be sent, together with the Objections, to the other House, by which it shall likewise be reconsidered, and if approved by two thirds of that House, it shall become a Law. But in all such Cases the Votes of both Houses shall be determined by Yeas and Nays, and the Names of the Persons voting for and against the Bill shall be entered on the Journal of each House respectively. If any Bill shall not be returned by the President within ten Days (Sundays excepted) after it shall have been presented to him, the Same shall be a Law, in like Manner as if he had signed it, unless the Congress by their Adjournment prevent its Return, in which Case it shall not be a Law.

Every Order, Resolution, or Vote to which the Concurrence of the Senate and House of Representatives may be necessary (except on a question of Adjournment) shall be presented to the President of the United States; and before the Same shall take Effect, shall be approved by him, or being disapproved by him, shall be repassed by two thirds of the Senate and House of Representatives, according to the Rules and Limitations prescribed in the Case of a Bill.

SECTION 8. The Congress shall have Power To lay and collect Taxes, Duties, Imposts and Excises, to pay the Debts and provide for the common Defence and general Welfare of the United States; but all Duties, Imposts and Excises shall be uniform throughout the United States;

To borrow money on the credit of the United States;

To regulate Commerce with foreign Nations, and among the several States, and with the Indian Tribes;

To establish an uniform Rule of Naturalization, and uniform Laws on the subject of Bankruptcies throughout the United States;

To coin Money, regulate the Value thereof, and of foreign Coin, and fix the Standard of Weights and Measures;

To provide for the Punishment of counterfeiting the Securities and current Coin of the United States;

To establish Post Offices and post Roads;

To promote the Progress of Science and useful Arts, by securing for limited Times to Authors and Inventors the exclusive Right to their respective Writings and Discoveries;

To constitute Tribunals inferior to the supreme Court;

To define and punish Piracies and Felonies committed on the high Seas, and Offenses against the Law of Nations;

*chuse – old spelling

The preamble to the United States Constitution contains the words ". . . to promote the general welfare." This is the foundation of the American welfare state.

Left: *Under the leadership of Chancellor Otto von Bismarck (1815–1898), Germany became the first modern welfare state. He initiated programs that provided health and accident insurance and old-age pensions to workers.*
Above: *Manufacture of steel tubing at the National Pipe Works in McKeesport, Pennsylvania. The industrial revolution created unprecedented wealth for some, while workers labored for low wages in often dangerous occupations.*

The Great Depression affected people in all regions of the country. Right: A migrant family looking for work in the cotton fields of the American southwest. This photo was taken by Dorothea Lange in 1937. Below: Shantytown in New York City.

Franklin Delano Roosevelt sought to pull the American economy out of the Great Depression by offering a "New Deal" of government-sponsored jobs programs and new social welfare legislation. One of the notable successes of his administration was the passage of the Social Security Act of 1935, which created old-age pensions for retired workers and required states to establish unemployment insurance programs.

The WPA was a New Deal agency that gave work to an estimated 8 million unemployed workers, including many artists, writers, and theater people. Here a WPA artist works on a sketch of a mural.
Facing page, top: *Another New Deal agency was the Tennessee Valley Authority. It undertook to tame one of America's wildest waterways, the Tennessee River. The TVA put thousands to work building power and flood-control dams like this one near Knoxville.*
Facing page, bottom: *The Truman administration built on the Roosevelt legacy with a program called the "Fair Deal." The Fair Deal included massive federal aid for housing. In this 1945 photo, "homesteaders" patiently wait outside the Federal Housing Authority office in Los Angeles to obtain federal housing "priorities" for low-cost homes.*

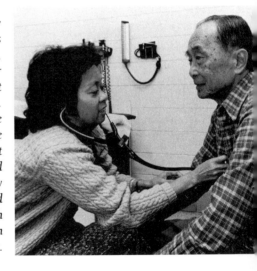

Top: *One of the key
programs of Lyndon Johnson's
"Great Society" was Medicare,
which helps people over
the age of sixty-five meet
their medical costs.
Here Johnson signs the
Medicare bill while the
elderly former president
Harry Truman (seated) and
Vice President Hubert Humphrey
look on. Truman had
proposed a national health
care insurance program
nearly twenty years earlier.*

Bottom: *Doctor examines a senior citizen in Boston.*

Riot scene in Detroit, 1967. Some people blamed the civil disturbances of the 1960s on the "Great Society." They argued that its programs had raised expectations to an impossible-to-meet level.

Sioux children in Red Shirt Village, South Dakota, say the
Pledge of Allegiance. They are in a Head Start program,
a Great Society early-childhood education program that
even many conservatives consider a success.

Trade unionists rally for national health insurance.
Health care policy has become a high priority
on the national agenda.

*The 1980s saw a huge increase in the homeless population
and renewed debate on the nation's housing needs.*

The "Reagan Revolution" of the 1980s was a
conservative movement to cut taxes and reduce
government spending on social programs.

Above: *Scene at an income maintenance (welfare) center.
Given the bureaucratic hassles that must be endured, it is hard
to believe that anyone would willingly choose to be on welfare.
But many critics of the welfare system make that contention.*

Facing page, bottom: *"We are angry and bored with the lies
and stereotypes about moms who depend on government child
support (AFDC). We will no longer remain silent." So reads the
mission statement of the* Welfare Mothers Voice, *a newspaper
published by Welfare Warriors.*

Groups like the Welfare Warriors in Milwaukee, Wisconsin, advocate for the rights of people on public assistance. Here moms fight to stop a proposal by the governor to cut the state's AFDC (Aid to Families with Dependent Children) benefits by 6 percent.

Street scene in the South Bronx, New York City. Some see the South Bronx as a symbol of the failure of the good intentions of social welfare programs. Others believe government did not truly commit itself to making these programs work.

created are in companies that don't provide pension plans.[8] More and more, it seems, Social Security is becoming a kind of permanent welfare, providing for millions of Americans from the time they retire until the time they die.

Major Federal Welfare Programs

THE welfare state is an enormous—and enormously complicated—structure. As we have seen, it involves not only those relief programs that people usually think of as "welfare," but the whole range of programs and agencies that provide government assistance to people.

Most broadly defined, the welfare state includes many programs that benefit middle class and wealthy Americans as well as those that benefit the poor. It includes Social Security, which goes to all retired people whatever their other income or total wealth. It includes government grants to universities, which help universities provide opportunities for students from all social classes. It even includes the tax deduction given to home owners for the interest on their mortgages, which makes it easier for middle- and upper-class people to afford bigger and better homes.

But, even a more limited definition includes a bewildering variety of welfare state programs—too many to deal with in any detail here. Probably the most common definition of a welfare program is one that provides cash or noncash benefits for persons with limited income. Even by that standard, there are over seventy federally sponsored welfare programs.[1] And that figure, large as it is, does not include the hundreds (if not thousands) of purely state, county, and city programs that offer goods and services to people in need.

The Structure of a Typical Welfare Program

Most national welfare programs are run by a combination of the federal, state, and local governments. Typically, the broad outline of the program is set by the federal government. The state then establishes its own version of the program within the federal guidelines. It is usually the state that decides what level of income will qualify a recipient for help and the exact amount of benefits he or she will receive.

The costs of these joint federal-state programs are shared. The federal contribution usually matches or exceeds the amount contributed by the states. In a recent year, all these programs together paid out about $173 billion in benefits, with 72.6 percent of the money coming from the national government.[2] If that figure included Social Security benefits, it would more than double, to over $413 billion, with a much higher proportion coming from the federal government.[3]

About half of ordinary welfare benefits are paid out directly in the form of cash payments, food benefits, or housing assistance. About 40 percent goes to pay for medical care. Most of the rest goes for educational and job programs, particularly job training.[4]

With so many programs, involving so many levels of government, it would be impossible to describe them all here. Instead, we will concentrate on a few of the biggest and most important social welfare programs.

Supplementary Security Income

Supplemental Security Income, or SSI, is a federal program that provides income to certain categories of people in need. SSI is administered by the Social Security Administration, but it is not a Social Security program. It is paid for out of general government revenues, not from the

Social Security trust fund. Also, it is available to people who have never worked and therefore have never paid any Social Security taxes.

SSI is different from Social Security in another important way as well. Unlike that much larger program, it is means-tested. That is, recipients must prove to the government that their financial situation is bad enough for them to need assistance.

SSI recipients must have a low current income, and less than $2,000 (if single), or $3,000 (if a couple) in assets. Assets include cash money, bank accounts, investments, real estate, precious jewelry, or other objects of special monetary value. Ordinarily assets don't include a recipient's home, clothes, household furniture, or car. The asset limit is set by the federal government and is the same across the country. The income limit varies from state to state.

In addition, a person must fit into one of three categories to qualify for SSI: she or he must be either elderly (over sixty-five), or legally blind, or disabled. Persons of any age qualify as disabled if they are seriously mentally retarded, or if they have a physical or mental disease that will keep them from working for at least twelve months or that is expected to kill them.

There are certain restrictions. In general, people who live in a public institution (prison, hospital, government-run nursing home, etc.) are not eligible. Nor are those who are unwilling to take vocational training if it is offered to them.

As of late 1990, the federal SSI benefit for an individual was $386 per month, for a couple $579. This is below the federal poverty line.[5] Not everyone gets even this much, however. Benefits are lower whenever the recipient has another source of income, however small. Benefits can also be reduced if the recipient's spouse or parent (if the recipient is a child) has an income. Some states supplement the federal SSI benefits, but only four supplement it enough to raise the recipient's income over the poverty level.

In most states, people who get SSI are automatically eligible for Medicaid as well. In many states they are also eligible for other services, such as food stamps, low-income housing assistance, state-supported housekeeping and home-care services, when these are available.

Medicaid

Medicaid is a joint federal-state-local program that provides medical care to poor people who are unable to qualify for Medicare. Although the federal government supplies more than half the funds for Medicaid, the individual states decide how the program will operate within their borders. Local agencies are often responsible for administering much of the program.

In most states, anyone receiving SSI is automatically eligible for Medicaid as well. Beyond that, each state sets its own income limits for Medicaid eligibility, as well as its own standards for services. Because of this, a person may be eligible for Medicaid in one state and not in another. What's more, Medicaid may pay for certain services in one state and not in another.

In most states, Medicaid pays for most of the same services paid for by Medicare, and in some states it pays for more. It is even possible for some people to belong to both programs at once.

In general, Medicaid is free to those who have little or no income, although in some states recipients toward the top of the poverty scale may be charged a small fee.

Aid to Families with Dependent Children (AFDC)

Aid to Families with Dependent Children (AFDC) is the program most people think of when someone mentions "welfare." It is the government's main effort to help children whose parents cannot afford to fully provide for them financially.

In 1990, a record 4.029 million families signed up for AFDC. They included a total of 11.6 million people, 7.9 million of whom were children. In 1991, officials estimated that AFDC would pay out about $18.5 billion in benefits, $9.9 billion of which would come from the federal government, and the rest from the states.[6]

Roughly 98 percent of the children who benefit from AFDC have two living parents, although about half have parents who are not, or never were, married. Whether married or not, in most cases, the parents are not living together. Almost nine out of ten (88 percent) live with one parent, in most cases their mother.

In many cases, this is because the parents don't get along. In others, it is because one parent is in prison or confined to a hospital of some kind. But another factor is the reluctance of many states to grant benefits for children with two parents at home, especially if either of them has a job. Unfortunately, this reluctance encourages poor families to break up, because that is often the only way the children are eligible to receive aid.

A program called AFDC-UP (AFDC for Unemployed Parents) tries to offset this pressure, and make it economically practical for poor families to stay together. It extends AFDC assistance to low-income, two-parent families when the main breadwinner is unemployed, or only able to work less than a hundred hours a month.

Until recently, states could elect to adopt AFDC-UP or not, and many decided not to in order to save money. Now, however, all states have been required to offer AFDC-UP. Even so, states are forbidden to provide AFDC to two-parent families in which either parent has a full-time job, no matter how little money they make.[7]

Almost 11 million families with at least one working parent do receive help under the federal Earned Income Tax Credits (EITC) program. EITC offers a cash supplement to intact families with working parents who still can't climb over the poverty line.

AFDC benefits vary widely from state to state, and sometimes even from place to place within a state. In general, benefits are somewhat higher in areas where rents and living costs are relatively high, and less where they are low. In Wisconsin, which has been relatively generous in the past, the most a single parent with one child can receive is $440 a month.[8]

Nationally, benefits are expected to average about $393 in 1991, which is actually down a little from $402 in constant (adjusted-for-inflation) dollars the year before.

AFDC families are usually also entitled to benefits from other programs. In most states, these include food stamps, free school meals for the children in school, home heating assistance, and, most significantly, Medicaid. No one can receive both AFDC and SSI benefits, although blind or disabled children may receive SSI payments while others in their family receive AFDC.

Other Programs to Help Children

AFDC is not the only major program aimed at children. The Women, Infants, and Children program (WIC) helps provide food to over 4 million low-income pregnant women, nursing mothers, infants, and children every month.

Head Start prepares preschool children from low-income families to enter elementary school. Head Start is probably the least controversial of all the social welfare programs. In 1991, President George Bush set a goal of getting all poor children into the program by 1994, and called for a $100 million increase in the program's budget for 1992. This was widely applauded as a noble goal, but a major children's advocacy group called the Children's Defense Fund estimate that it would take a $2.3 billion increase—or twenty-three times that much!—to actually achieve.[9]

The federal school lunch program provides lunches,

and in some places breakfasts, to children from low-income families on school days. On the average, about 11.7 million children eat at least one nourishing meal subsidized by a federal grant every day schools are open.

Food Stamps

Most government food benefits are distributed through food stamps. These are coupons, each of which has a spendable value. They are like a special kind of money that can be spent only for food. In 1989, the food stamp program distributed more than twice as much food to low-income Americans as WIC and the school lunch programs combined.

The basic principle behind the program is a simple one. No one in America should be allowed to starve, or to become seriously malnourished and ill because they don't have enough money to buy food.

Over 16 million Americans get food stamps every year. About 98 percent of all the benefits go to people with incomes below the official poverty line, and about 83 percent to families with children.[10]

Like SSI, AFDC, and Medicaid, the food stamps program is means-tested. The size of a person's food stamp benefit depends on his or her income. Ordinarily, a single person must have a gross income (before any payroll deductions or taxes) of no more than $8,172 a year to qualify for any help at all. For a couple, the limit is $10,956. For a family of four, it is $16,512. Exceptions are made for people with slightly higher incomes if they are elderly or disabled and are eligible for Social Security. Those who receive SSI, on the other hand, cannot receive food stamps at all. That is because the SSI benefits include a grant for food.

The maximum value of food stamps an individual can receive is $105 a month. For a couple, the maximum is $193, and for a family of four, $352. Only about 18 percent of all recipients receive the maximum amount of food stamps, however. The benefits that most people actually receive add up to about 95¢ a meal.[11]

Food stamps are as much a way of helping the nation's farming, food processing, and food sales industries as they are of helping the poor. They create an important market for all these industries, pumping over $10 billion into them every year.

Other Welfare Programs

The big programs described in this chapter are supplemented by hundreds of smaller federal, state, county, city, and private programs and agencies. They range from Wisconsin's Learnfare program that requires AFDC parents to force their children to attend school every day or lose their benefits, to community food pantries that hand out canned goods to people who cannot afford to feed themselves.

But the fact that there are so many social welfare programs does not mean that everyone who needs help is getting it. Millions of poor Americans still fall through the holes in the safety net. Millions more are caught by the net, only to find themselves entangled there, and unable to free themselves.

Living on Welfare

WHO are the people who actually use the programs described in the previous chapter? Who are the millions of Americans who are, as it is sometimes put, living on welfare?

Welfare recipients are almost as varied as the American population itself. They come in all colors, shapes, and sizes, from all religious and ethnic backgrounds. The only thing that they have in common is economic need.

They are ordinary Americans who had the bad luck to be born poor or severely disabled.

They are middle class people who have met some form of personal or economic disaster.

They are families whose breadwinners lost their jobs because the companies they worked for went bankrupt.

They are veterans of World War II, Korea, Vietnam, and Desert Storm who were never able to adjust to life after the horrors of war.

They are teenage young women who got pregnant, and whose boyfriends would not take any responsibility for the children.

They are women and men whose spouses died or deserted them, and left them with children to raise and no way to support them alone.

They are women who left their marriages because their

75

husbands beat them, or beat or sexually abused their children. They are the children who suffered that abuse.

Life can be a nightmare for people who rely on the welfare system for their main, or only, source of income. Economic survival can be a daily challenge. Surviving emotionally and spiritually can be even harder. Raising healthy, well-adjusted children can be nearly impossible.

Finances

Typical single welfare parents with two children in Milwaukee, Wisconsin receive $517 a month. Out of that, they must pay: Milwaukee's big-city rents; regular heat, light, water, and sewer bills; clothing expenses for the children and themselves; transportation for the children to and from school, and for themselves to and from the welfare office, job interviews, doctor's offices, and anywhere else they need to go; and all the other expenses that are regular obligations of modern life.

The average poor family pays about 55 percent of its total income on housing, and another 33 percent on food (about 68¢ a meal).[1] For a Milwaukee AFDC family, that leaves a grand total of $62.04 a month to meet all the other expenses that are bound to arise.

One of the biggest of those expenses, for many families, is day care. For most families on welfare, professional day care can be hard to find and impossible to afford. Ironically, the day care problem is biggest for those welfare parents who are trying to work their way out of the system. In theory, both the federal government and many states help provide day care for welfare parents who are attempting to work. But in reality this help is not always available.

When a family is trying to get by on $517 a month, the loss of a child's shoe can be a disaster. There is simply no money to buy a new pair of shoes—and no credit card either, even if the family could afford to pay interest. And how can a child go to school without shoes? Food stamps, medical care, and other benefits help. But, for most welfare families, the figures never add up. The amount of the benefit never pays for all the family needs.

Jumping Through the Hoops

One of the most constant frustrations of life on welfare is the need to deal with the welfare bureaucracy. For many welfare recipients, it seems that half their lives are spent filling out forms, explaining themselves to social workers, and arguing with bureaucrats to get the meager benefits they're entitled to receive.

According to Pat Gowans, the head of a Milwaukee-based advocacy group called Welfare Warriors, just enrolling in the AFDC program can be a major ordeal. Some applicants have to spend a whole day in the welfare office, and sometimes two, before even getting the opportunity to apply.

The process involves filling out a complicated thirty-seven-page form which, Gowans says, is written in language appropriate for a college sophomore, even though many applicants never finished high school.[2] An applicant who is unable to understand the form can get help, but it is often given in a contemptuous manner by a welfare office employee who is overworked, irritable, and unsympathetic.

In addition to filling out the form, the applicant has to produce a wide range of documentation: Social Security numbers for every family member, birth certificates for each child, household bills, and other things that she or he may find hard to locate. Those who have trouble producing the documents are sometimes made to feel ignorant and incompetent. Or worse, they are treated with suspicion, as likely cheaters who are trying to put something over on the welfare system.

To add to the frustration, the whole demeaning process has to be repeated over and over again, every six months, as long as the family stays on welfare. Even the same birth certificates, for the same children, have to be hauled back to the welfare office—as though the children's births would somehow have changed over the past six months.

Some AFDC recipients are also required to show repeated proof that they are looking for a job. In Milwaukee, some parents are made to appear regularly at the welfare office to make phone calls asking for a job. Frustratingly, they are forbidden to call employers who are currently advertising for workers. That, they are told, would put them into direct competition with non-welfare job seekers.[3]

The need for some formal procedures is obvious. But it is hard for welfare recipients to see the need for the barrage of forms and petty requirements the bureaucracy keeps firing at them. They feel like circus animals, forced to jump through hoops when the ringmaster cracks the whip. Welfare activists like Pat Gowans believe that it is a form of harassment, deliberately built into the system to make them pay, in frustration and humiliation, for every bit of help they receive.

Stigma

The disdainful treatment welfare applicants get at the welfare office is only the beginning. Once enrolled, adults and children alike bear the social stigma that attaches to welfare families.

Many middle-class Americans are strongly prejudiced against welfare recipients. They see them as freeloaders who use the tax money of middle-class Americans to support a life of idleness and waste. Their prejudice is fueled by misunderstanding and exaggerated by racial prejudice. Most middle-class Americans are white, and they think of people on welfare as being almost entirely black. In fact, however, most welfare recipients are white.

Most middle-class people have no understanding of

what life on welfare can be like. The gap between middle-class expectations and the reality of life on welfare can be enormous. Middle-class people are often appalled, for example, to learn that some young welfare mothers buy disposable diapers.

A judge once lectured a mother from the bench for being so extravagant. But, the mother protested, her baby needed constant changing. What could she do? Buy cloth diapers, snorted the judge, and wash them between changings. But I have no washing machine. Go to the laundromat. But my neighborhood doesn't have a laundromat, and it would cost me even more to travel across town. Well, wash the diapers in the sink. But I have no hot water. There's no way to sterilize them. Well, said the exasperated judge, whenever the baby needs a change, tear up some old bedsheets. The mother was stunned. Did this comfortable, self-righteous, well-off middle-class man really think she had *more than one sheet?*

Pat Gowans speaks of the "hate" that welfare recipients often feel from their more fortunate neighbors. It is a strong word, but not too strong to describe the way some people feel about those on welfare.

One rural midwestern resident felt so strongly that he wrote his local newspaper to vent his anger. "I swallow a bitter taste," he wrote, "when I see illegal aliens who cannot speak our language plunk down $50 worth of food stamps for a cart of groceries. I'm careful to drive around the local welfare office. I've been sickened too many times by unkempt girls in baggy blue jeans with baby on the hip awaiting the weekly dole."[4]

Much of this hostility is born in ignorance and prejudice. The letter writer, for example, knew nothing about the personal circumstances of any of the people he wrote about. What's more, he almost certainly had some key facts wrong. (Illegal immigrants would not be eligible for food stamps, for instance.) But the hostility is real, and it has a chilling effect on the people who have to face it every day.

And there is almost no way to avoid facing it. It is almost impossible to keep the fact that you receive welfare private. Recipients are singled out publicly in a number of ways. Some banks, in cities like Milwaukee and San Diego, have separate lines for cashing welfare checks.[5] Standing in this line broadcasts the fact that one is on welfare to everyone in the bank.

The embarrassment many welfare recipients feel comes to a head in the checkout line of the supermarket, when they have to pull out food stamps in full view of everyone in line. The use of what Pat Gowans calls this "play money" does more than mark the customers as welfare recipients. It opens them up to the ridicule of strangers. Other people in line often roll their eyes, or make cruel remarks. Even the grocery clerks sometimes exhibit disdain, if not outright hostility. Many AFDC mothers report being called "welfare slut" and worse by other customers, often in front of their horrified children.

The welfare stigma has a special sting for those who never dreamed that they would ever need public assistance. Often, they are people who once felt the same prejudice against welfare recipients themselves. As a Rancho Cucamonga, California, woman who found herself on welfare after leaving a husband who threatened her with a gun, expressed it to *The Ladies Home Journal* magazine, "I would stand in line, thinking, I'm different from these people. I am not going to do this forever." She was so embarrassed to be seen by people she knew that she "would go to a store at the other end of town to use my food stamps."[6]

But the effects of the welfare stigma are hardest of all on the children. Many children of families who receive help from welfare grow up accustomed to seeing their own parents treated with disrespect, and worse, by social workers and strangers alike. It probably shouldn't be surprising, then, that many have little respect for their parents themselves. They grow up despising their own family, and therefore with a damaged sense of their own worth.

The Lost Children
A large proportion of welfare recipients live in poor inner-city neighborhoods or other places where life is difficult and dangerous. Many are homeless, or live in hovels that are little more than shacks. Others live in fire-trap high-rise tenements, where the elevators stick between floors, the stairways smell of urine, and the halls are always dark, because vandals keep breaking the lights and the landlord never repairs them. Rapes are common in those dark hallways, and murder is far from rare.

Living in such conditions can be destructive to individuals and families alike. It is hard enough on the adults; it can be death to the children. Youngsters in many poor neighborhoods have to detour around drug dealers on their way to kindergarten. Concerned parents give first graders instructions on what to do when they hear gunfire in the streets on their way home. It is hardly surprising that many of these children grow up damaged, either physically or emotionally.

Pat Gowans estimates that big-city welfare mothers "lose" one out of every three children: either to drugs, disease, prison, violent crime, or to the social welfare system itself.[7] Others think that may be a high estimate nationwide, but it could very well be true in some cities, and particularly in some neighborhoods.

Common Misconceptions
There is a widespread belief that people on welfare "have it easy." Everyone has heard fantastic stories of welfare mothers who buy caviar and filet mignon with food stamps at the local supermarket, and "welfare queens" who ride

up to the welfare office in brand-new Cadillacs. Such stories are so unlikely that most people discount them. Still, a doubt often remains.

Even many who don't believe the myths of caviar and Cadillacs may accept other common misconceptions. One is the idea that many women keep having baby after baby to increase the amount they get from welfare. Another is the belief that most people on welfare choose to be there because it is easier than going to work. This may be true of some individuals, but anyone who's seen what welfare life is really like realizes that they are not typical. Certainly any woman who has children to increase her welfare benefits soon learns that she spends more on the child than the amount her payments are increased.

Life on welfare is never lavish. It is inevitably difficult and frustrating, and often humiliating as well. There is nothing "easy" about it.

The Welfare State Debate

THE United States has been committed to some form of national welfare system for more than fifty years. And yet, the nature of the welfare state is still the subject of intense debate.

To some, welfare is still a form of charity; to others, it is a right. And some critics still argue that there should be no welfare state at all.

Six Arguments Against the Welfare State (With Rebuttals)

Blanket opposition to any kind of welfare is a radical position held by only the most extreme economic conservatives. Even Ronald Reagan talked of helping the "truly needy," while Jack Kemp, President Bush's conservative Secretary of Housing and Urban Development, insists that "There is both a moral [and a] political obligation to combat poverty and despair."[1]

Yet, some descendants of the Social Darwinists still insist that the federal government has no business giving help to the poor and disadvantaged. They make at least six arguments they believe strike straight to the heart of the whole concept of the welfare state.

1. *The welfare state costs too much.* Probably the most

frequent complaint made about the welfare state is how expensive it is. In 1988, welfare programs cost the government $173 billion.[2] By 1991, the conservative Heritage Foundation was estimating welfare costs at "over $180 billion a year."[3]

Even this enormous amount of money adds up to less than $5,500 for every poor person in the country. That may not seem an unreasonable amount of money, *if* we assume that the government has the responsibility to lift everyone out of poverty. But it is far more, the critics say, than a country as deeply in debt as the United States can afford to spend.

Defenders of the welfare state respond that a civilized nation cannot afford *not* to spend whatever is needed to provide the necessities of life to its people. The nation's debt can be paid off in other ways—by cutting the defense budget, perhaps, or raising taxes. It would be unfeeling, and immoral, to pay off the national debt at the expense of the poorest, sickest, and weakest among us.

2. *The welfare state is a form of Big Brother.* Once the government assumes the role of providing for an individual's welfare, it assumes great power over that individual's life. Welfare regulations give the federal government the right, and even the duty, to pry into people's personal lives to determine whether they're eligible for assistance. And it's not just privacy that's at risk under the welfare state, say the critics. Personal liberties are threatened as well. Welfare can be used by the government as a tool to control people's lives, to bribe them, or coerce them, to do its will in order to get their welfare checks. This view was expressed by a committee of the U.S. Chamber of Commerce more than forty years ago: "The total drift of the welfare state is toward the concentration of power and authority," it concluded, "toward the total state—totalitarianism."[4]

As we will see, welfare clients often do need to surrender some privacy and independence. Nonetheless, defenders of the welfare state argue, the fear that welfare is the first step toward totalitarianism is overdone. After all, the United States has *been* a welfare state for half a century, and it is not totalitarian yet. Countries like Great Britain, Sweden, and Holland have been welfare states for even longer, and they are not totalitarian either.

3. *The welfare state is fundamentally opposed to the capitalist economic system that has made the American economy the richest in the world.* Some critics fear that even if the welfare state doesn't lead to totalitarianism, it will lead to socialism. And from there it is only a small step to communism, and finally to the destruction of the American economy and way of life.

But, argue the defenders of the welfare state, protecting the American way of life must not mean assuring the continuation of widespread poverty and suffering. Besides, the welfare state supporters say, socialism and communism are no longer serious threats since the collapse of communism in Eastern Europe. The real challenges to America's economy today come from Germany and Japan, two countries that have much more generous social welfare systems than the United States.

4. *It is wrong for the government to give away other people's money.* It may be noble to help the poor, some critics say, but that doesn't make it right for the government to steal from those who are not poor to do it. The welfare state government, these critics charge, acts as a kind of official Robin Hood. It robs from the rich and the middle class and gives to the poor. This, they protest, is morally wrong. If economically successful people want to give their own money to the poor, fine. But the government has no right to force them to do it by taxing them for that purpose.

Supporters of the welfare state respond that, far from being morally wrong, welfare is morally necessary. The Robin Hood argument, they say, is not really an argument against welfare, but a complaint against taxation in general. If it is wrong to tax people to help their fellow citizens, then it is wrong to tax them for any reason at all. That issue was settled in Article I Section VIII of the U.S. Constitution, which gives Congress "the power to lay and collect taxes . . . to . . . provide for the common defense and general welfare of the United States. . . ." "Besides," some defenders of the welfare state would add, "Robin Hood was a hero, wasn't he?"

5. *Welfare robs the poor of their initiative.* Welfare is supposed to help the poor and the disadvantaged. But in the long run, some critics complain, it does just the opposite. While it may meet their immediate needs for food and shelter, it robs them of something much more important. "The tragedy of relief," says Judge Juanita Kidd Stout, "is that it takes away from people the drive to work."[5] And Secretary of Housing and Urban Development Jack Kemp has complained that "Our welfare system basically is more of a trap, and not a springboard onto the ladder of opportunity."[6] Many Americans believe that once someone gets on welfare they tend to stay there for the rest of their lives. Critics of the system often complain of families who are on welfare for generation after generation.

Ex-Senator Barry Goldwater expressed another widely held belief when he wrote that "one of the great evils of welfarism," was the fact that "it transforms the individual from a dignified, industrious, self-reliant spiritual being into a dependent animal creature without his knowing it."[7]

Supporters of the welfare state find such statements outrageous. The people who receive welfare, they point out, are not "animal creatures." They are living, breathing human beings—with the same feelings, needs, and desires of everyone else, including United States Senators. They are elderly people, disabled workers, physically ill children, and loving mothers and fathers struggling to raise their children in some of the most desperate circumstances imaginable.

As for the complaint that welfare is a trap that ensnares people forever, welfare authorities report that very few people actually spend their lives on welfare. Many programs have limits on how long a person can receive benefits. The "trap" critics most often complain about is AFDC, where, according to a Congressional Research Bureau Report, the expected length of stay is "at least eight years."[8] That's longer than most welfare supporters would like it to be, but it is nothing like the lifetime on welfare the critics like to complain about.

As for those who do find it hard to escape welfare, the system's supporters say, society cannot just abandon them. It's all very well to say that people should be self-reliant, but before anyone can be self-reliant she or he needs to be fed and clothed.

Even Jack Kemp, who is a harsh critic of the current welfare system, rejects the idea that welfare should be abandoned altogether. "I have friends on the right who say, 'I pulled myself up by the bootstraps, why can't they?'" says Kemp. "It's pretty hard to pick yourself up by the bootstraps when you have no boots."[9]

6. *Welfare does not end poverty.* The most damning of all the criticisms of the welfare state is that welfare does not work. Critics argue that this is proved by the fact that the United States has been a welfare state for half a century and still has enormous numbers of poor people.

"In the sixties we waged a War on Poverty," says Ronald Reagan, "and poverty won."[10] Ever since, other critics of the welfare system argue, welfare spending and the number of poor people have gone up together. If we can keep spending more money on welfare without lowering the number of poor people, these critics ask, what good is it?

Supporters of the welfare state insist that these arguments are misleading. The fact that the War on Poverty did not totally eliminate poverty does not mean it did no good at all. In fact, they insist, it proved how effective social welfare programs can be.

In 1960, the last census before the War on Poverty was declared, there were almost 40 million poor people in the United States. By 1970, after the Great Society had been in place for less than a decade, that number was down to 25,400,000. And the massive social effort was most successful of all in helping those who needed it most. In the mid-1960s, the elderly were the poorest group in America. By 1974, thanks to programs like Medicare and Medicaid, they had lost that unwanted distinction.[11] Today, they have one of the lowest poverty rates of any group in society.

If welfare has failed to lower overall poverty in recent years, the defenders argue, it's because the past two presidential administrations have deliberately undermined its effectiveness. Presidents Reagan and Bush have tightened welfare regulations so much that millions of poor people don't even qualify for help. What's more, millions who do receive help don't get enough to keep them from being poor.

Overall welfare spending has not been rising because welfare programs have become more generous, say the welfare state's supporters. Spending has gone up because problems in the economy have caused millions of previously middle-class people to slip into poverty.

Is Welfare Charity?

Much of the debate over the welfare state assumes that welfare is a form of charity. It is seen as a way for the successful members of society to help those who are in need. Opponents of the welfare state argue that this should be the job of private individuals and organizations, not of the government. Supporters argue that the government is the only institution big enough, and responsible enough, to provide the amount of aid that is needed.

Clearly, welfare has some of its roots in the private charities of earlier times. But it has other roots as well. In England, the Poor Laws of the seventeenth century were established to reduce the number of beggars, and to keep the cutpurses under control. Bismarck first introduced his welfare measures in Germany to head off revolution, and then expanded them to prepare the German citizenry for war.

The fact is that welfare has never been intended *only* to help the poor. It has always been intended to benefit society at large. It is designed to do this in a variety of ways. Some of them involve the kinds of social engineering its critics often complain about.

According to Frances Fox Piven and Richard A. Cloward, in their book *Regulating the Poor*, "The key to an understanding of relief-giving is in the functions it serves for the larger economic and political order . . . expansive relief policies are designed to mute civil disorder, and restrictive ones to reinforce work norms."[12]

In other words, the welfare state is sometimes used not just to help the poor, but to control them. When masses of people are condemned to poverty and living without hope, they are apt to become desperate. They turn to drugs, alcohol, and crime in much greater numbers than other people. The result is soaring crime rates, increased need for police and prisons, and a general deterioration of the nation's quality of life. So, when jobs are scarce, and discontent boils up among the poor and unemployed, welfare benefits are often raised. This acts to quiet the discontent, and to lessen the chance that large numbers of desperate people will turn to crime and other forms of antisocial behavior.

When times are better and there are more jobs that need filling, welfare requirements are tightened. This encourages people to try harder to get off welfare and to snap up the available jobs. This is partially what happened in the United States in the 1980s, when many low-wage jobs appeared in the economy.

But not all social engineering is so cold-blooded. One of the welfare state's main goals is to improve what economists call the stock of human capital. A nation's people are its most valuable resource. It is the people who create the nation's civilization, and who produce, buy, maintain, and consume the nation's goods. Therefore, the better fed, housed, and educated the general population is, the more prosperous the nation is likely to be.

By helping the millions of people who are poor and disadvantaged improve their own lot, welfare improves the quality of life for everyone. This is particularly true of those welfare programs directed toward the young. "[Such programs are] not charity," argued a recent editorial in the *Miami Herald*, "but building for the common good. It is in our interest and our country's interest to invest in the health of every baby, in a good start for low-income preschoolers, in everyone's children moving through school and into further education or training for work with a future."[13]

On the most obvious level, children who get a good education, and who grow up to get a good job, will not require further government spending on welfare benefits. Nor will they require nearly as much in the way of medical care. But lower future health and welfare costs are just some of the tremendous savings society hopes to reap by providing help for the poor and disadvantaged.

An uneducated and untrained population means an uneducated and untrained work force. This is a tremendous national disadvantage in the economic competition with other countries, such as Germany and Japan. This is the reason many leading business figures often support key welfare-state measures. As the heads of five major U.S.

corporations recently declared in a joint statement calling for expanding the food supplement program, "The health, well-being and education of children in the United States are pivotal to keeping the United States competitive in an increasingly international economy."[14]

For all the reasons discussed here, it is a mistake to think of welfare primarily as a charity, or as a way to help the poor. But if welfare is more than charity, what else is it?

Is There a Right to Welfare?

Some people argue that welfare is a positive moral and political right, perhaps even a constitutional right. Senator (later Vice-President) Hubert Humphrey made this argument when he stated that "The welfare state has been an American objective ever since the Constitution was adopted one hundred and fifty years ago."[15] In Humphrey's view, the welfare state is the logical outgrowth of the Constitution's call for government "to promote the General Welfare."

But if that is so, opponents of the welfare state argue, why did it take so long for the government to establish what we now think of as welfare measures? The reason, according to Humphrey, was that for a long time "economic opportunity was open to all." In the modern world, however, that is no longer true.

"Today," Humphrey wrote in 1950, "millions of families are dependent on jobs that may disappear tomorrow through no fault of their own. Millions of families . . . barely eke out subsistence as they live on tiny, worn out farms which cannot produce decent livings. . . ."[16] And that reality has only gotten worse in the years since Humphrey wrote about it.

If Humphrey was correct, then welfare is the fulfillment of a promise made in the Constitution itself. In that sense, at least, it can be regarded as a constitutional right.

Opponents of the welfare state strongly disagree. They point out that the writers of the Constitution did not use the term "welfare" in the modern sense. They argue that the founders only meant the government should consider the well-being of the whole society in forming and carrying out its policies. They did not mean to suggest that the government should actually contribute to the economic well-being of individuals.

For most of the country's history, the courts tended to agree with this argument. They rejected the idea that the Constitution called for public assistance for the poor. In fact, it has been commented that "Public assistance in general was greatly restricted by a political philosophy of laissez-faire which considered major public aid to the poor by the Federal Government to be not only bad judgement but unconstitutional."[17]

But court judgements change. In 1970, the Supreme Court itself suggested that Humphrey might have been right. The majority opinion in a case known as *Goldberg v. Kelly* made the same direct link between the Constitution and the welfare state that Humphrey had made twenty years earlier.

> *"From its founding," the Court declared, "the Nation's basic commitment has been to foster the dignity and well-being of all persons within its borders. We have come to recognize that forces not within the control of the poor contribute to their poverty. This perception, against the background of our traditions, has significantly influenced the development of the contemporary public assistance system. Welfare, by meeting the demands of subsistence, can help bring within the reach of the poor the same opportunities that are available to others to participate meaningfully in the life of the community. At the same time, welfare guards against the societal malaise that may flow from a widespread sense of frustration and insecurity. Public assistance,*

then, is not mere charity, but a means to 'promote the General Welfare, and secure the Blessings of Liberty to ourselves and our Posterity.' "[18]

In other words, Humphrey was right.

The Need for Reform

ONLY the most radical critics of the welfare state call for abandoning the idea of welfare altogether. But that doesn't mean that anyone is happy with the welfare system as it currently exists. In fact, almost no one is.

"Everyone hates the current welfare system," says Harvard professor David Ellwood. "The conservatives think it breeds dependency. The liberals think it stigmatizes, isolates and doesn't provide enough income."[1] And no one hates it more than the welfare recipients themselves. They are the ones who suffer most from the defects in the system.

Virtually everyone would agree that the welfare system, as it exists today, is wasteful, inefficient, overly complex, and not nearly as effective as it ought to be. Although the critics disagree bitterly about what should be done to reform the present system, no one doubts that it is in need of reform.

Waste and Inefficiency

Everyone agrees that the current welfare system is inefficient, but it is hard to determine just how inefficient it actually is. According to an estimate given at a 1990 Conservative Leadership Conference, however, only 30 percent of the money spent on welfare gets to the people it is intended to help.[2] Most of the other 70 percent, conservatives and liberals would agree, is wasted.

If the Conservative Leadership Conference's figures are correct—or even close to correct—the bureaucratic costs are shockingly high. Speakers at the Conference pointed out that this compares to only 20 percent administrative and bureaucratic costs for the international assistance program UNICEF, and about 30 to 33 percent in the *most* inefficient of the other UN agencies.

The conservatives complain most loudly about that part of the bureaucratic expenses paid to "bleeding-heart" social workers and other professionals. Liberals object most strongly to the amount spent to enforce "nit-picking" regulations, and trying to prove that potential recipients are really ineligible for help. Both would agree that far too much of the welfare budget goes to middle- and upper-level administrators.

While almost everyone agrees that there is enormous waste, one complaint many people make seems to be largely inaccurate. There is a widespread belief that a high proportion of welfare recipients are cheats. This impression is fostered by politicians who use welfare fraud as a campaign issue. Both Ronald Reagan and George Bush campaigned against so-called "welfare queens," who supposedly live lives of luxury on large amounts of money bilked out of various welfare programs. So have many other local, state, and national politicians.

Despite the fact that this charge is very widely believed, it seems to have little basis in reality. Even before welfare enforcement was stepped up under Reagan, the Department of Health, Education, and Welfare reported that "[s]uspected incidents of fraud or misrepresentation among welfare recipients occur in less than four-tenths of one per cent of the total welfare case load in the nation." Another 1 or 2 percent of recipients are "technically ineligible" because of misunderstandings or mistakes by welfare workers. But "[t]hese are human and technical errors," a Department publication insisted. "[I]t is not cheating."[3]

Some critics suggest there is probably more cheating today than there used to be, if only because there are more rules. Since it's easier to lose benefits, people are more inclined to fudge or withhold information from the welfare office. But most of whatever new cheating may be brought on by the stricter rules is probably minor—failing to disclose small amounts of outside earnings, or to report that a relative has moved in with a family on AFDC. Most knowledgeable observers doubt that there are actually many people on the welfare rolls who don't deserve to be there. Certainly there are very few, if any, who live luxurious lives on welfare benefits.

Complexity

One reason the welfare system is so inefficient is that it is so complex. There are so many programs, run by so many agencies, with so little coordination between them. It's difficult for anyone to make sense of it all, much less to administer it fairly.

As far back as 1972, the chairman of a Congressional subcommittee on fiscal policy summarized the welfare system this way: "We've ended up with so many programs that they can't be run well. Some people are left out while others scoop up thousands—far more than we could possibly provide to everyone. . . . And no one is in charge of all this."[4] Current critics say it hasn't gotten any better.

If the head of a congressional subcommittee can't make sense of the system, how can the people who are expected to run it? In 1990, a public interest group phoned Social Security offices in eighteen cities, and asked identical questions about the SSI program. They got a bewildering variety of answers. Many of the answers were confusing, often discouraging, and sometimes flat-out wrong. For example, even though Social Security offices are supposed to handle applications for SSI benefits, Social

Security workers in many places turned applicants away, telling them they needed to go to state welfare offices to apply.[5]

If the people who actually run the system can't understand it, how can the people who need to use it? All too often, they can't. A 1990 report, prepared for a group of social work and educational agencies, described the obstacles faced by a young client entering the system as "overwhelming." "[T]o expect a youth in crisis, or his or her overstressed parents to negotiate, unassisted, the maze of agencies, programs, and eligibility rules in order to get the help they need is truly to ask the impossible."[6] The same could be said for the elderly, the disabled, and others who need the system's help, but who have no training or experience that would help them to make sense of it.

Ineffectiveness

The current system might be forgiven some of its faults if it performed the services it was designed to perform for the people it is intended to serve. But, far too often, it does not.

"Leaving aside such obviously successful programs as Head Start and magnet schools," says the columnist William Raspberry, "most programs designed to help the poor aren't working very well."[7] Many supporters of the welfare system—as well as all its enemies—would agree.

Liberals are particularly upset that current welfare programs don't reach many of the people they should serve. According to the Children's Defense Fund, "Only about half of all Americans who are eligible for food stamps receive them."[8] Between 3 and 4 million low-income working families are likely to miss out on a $935 grant under the Earned Income Tax Credit program in 1991 simply because they don't know they are entitled to it.[9] And only about half the people eligible for SSI benefits actually receive them, according to Representative Edgar Roybal, the chairman of the House Select Committee on Aging.[10]

Goals for Reform

Everyone admits that reform is needed, and there is no shortage of suggestions for change. Welfare rights advocates continually press for increases in federal assistance for low-income housing construction, and expansion of such popular programs as Head Start, WIC, and food stamps. More conservative reformers tend to press for ways to simplify welfare programs, to restrict the numbers of people they serve, and to reduce the size of the bureaucracy that administers them.

While there is great debate over specific reforms, most would-be reformers agree on certain broad goals:

To reduce poverty in the United States. This is one of the ultimate goals of the welfare state. Any reforms, therefore should try to assure that programs either supply enough aid to raise recipients above the poverty level directly, or enough resources to help them become productive and self-supporting.

To encourage work. No one wants anyone to spend their entire lives on welfare. Ultimately, the only way poor families will be able to survive off welfare will be for one or more family members to find and keep a decent job. Welfare measures can do this in various ways: by educating welfare recipients so that they will qualify for a job, by helping them to find one, by caring for their children while they work, and by assuring that any work they get will be economically profitable for them.

To eliminate dependency on welfare. Most people would agree with Republican Senator Arlen Specter of Pennsylvania "that welfare is necessary for some people, but . . . [the system] ought to be constructed to move people [off it] as soon as possible."[11]

To keep families together. One of the great tragedies of modern poverty is that it puts enormous strain on families. Current welfare policies add to the strain by cutting benefits to families in which anyone is employed, no matter how little they make. This means that it is often economically more sensible for employed fathers (or, more rarely, mothers) to leave their spouse and children than to stay with them. Most people agree that it would be good to eliminate this kind of strain, and to make it more profitable for families to stay together than to fly apart.

To reduce waste, inefficiency, and fraud. Misspent welfare funds cost everyone—taxpayers and welfare recipients alike.

Ideas for Reform

ALTHOUGH many people would agree on the broad goals for welfare reform, there is little agreement about how to achieve them.

Conservatives tend to favor reforms that reduce government spending on welfare. Being deeply suspicious about the value of welfare in general, they tend to feel that the less money risked on it the better. Liberals, on the other hand, tend to favor reforms that would increase the flow of benefits to clients.

Tighten Eligibility Rules?

Some people favor making eligibility rules even stricter than they are now, and toughening means testing on virtually every public-assistance program. They argue that this would drastically reduce the number of people getting welfare, saving the taxpayers enormous amounts of money. At the same time, it would assure that the most desperate of the poor still receive help.

Some people would favor applying a kind of morality test as well as a means test. These are the descendants of the nineteenth-century charity-givers who would help only the "deserving" poor. They would drop people from welfare programs who indulge in socially unacceptable behavior. This might include women who continue to have children when they can't afford to pay for the ones they have; criminals; drug and alcohol abusers, who only need help because they are too drunk, or too stoned, to hold a job.

It is one thing, these reformers say, for society to support those who are too poor, too disabled, or too unfortunate to help themselves. But it is another thing to pay for those whose troubles are their own fault. Why should hardworking, taxpaying members of society be forced to pay to support people in the kind of immoral, and sometimes criminal, life-style that undermines society itself?

Eliminate Means Testing?

While some people want to tighten eligibility rules, others want to eliminate them altogether. They argue that a true welfare state can only be constructed on a foundation of benefits available to everybody, regardless of their need. They point to countries like Sweden, where every citizen is entitled to a wide range of benefits that guarantee a decent standard of living, regardless of their private income.

The case for this kind of welfare state was made by Sweden's Prime Minister Olaf Palme in a lecture at Harvard University: "An efficient and stable welfare state," Palme insisted, "must be based on universal social programs, such as health insurance, pensions, and child support allowances—programs extended to *all* citizens."[1]

Palme pointed out that this kind of system has several important advantages over the kinds of means-tested programs common in the United States. Means tests, he argued, only "encourage taxpayers to think in terms of 'us' and 'them.'" Eliminating them promotes "social solidarity." It removes the stigma from welfare recipients, and reduces the hostility that more prosperous taxpayers feel toward welfare in general.

"The fact is that it is not the weight of the tax burden that causes [hostility toward welfare] but rather the feeling among taxpayers that they do not get anything for their money. People who derive some benefit from a welfare system are its greatest supporters and will pay taxes without feeling exploited." Americans can understand this point by considering the very different public attitudes towards AFDC, which is means-tested, and Social Security, which is available to everybody.

Eliminating means testing has other benefits as well, Palme argued. It should appeal to conservatives, because making programs universal reduces the need for a large federal bureaucracy to enforce eligibility standards. What's more, it "would help eliminate the 'poverty trap,' in which the poor are discouraged from increasing their earnings, since to do so decreases their benefits."[2]

Spend More on Children?

Some of the most seriously debated welfare reforms involve AFDC and other programs designed to help children. Welfare rights advocates complain that the United States does a terrible job in looking after its children, particularly its poor children.

According to *Children 1990: A Report Card*, put out by the Children's Defense Fund, "As the wealthiest nation on Earth, and the standard-bearer of Democracy, we have an 'A' capacity to care for our children, and an 'F' performance."[3] Despite the wealth of the United States, its children have the highest poverty rate of children in the eight leading industrial nations.

The United States spends a lower proportion of its gross national product on childhood health measures than eighteen other industrialized nations. It ranks only a poor nineteenth among nations in the proportion of children who die before their first birthday, and a shocking thirtieth in the world in the mortality rate for black infants.[4] Some reformers argue that we need to increase the money that goes into virtually all the child-related programs.

Pat Gowans, of Welfare Warriors, believes that welfare

should be designed to support single parents who want to stay home and raise their children. She would extend this principle to anyone who gives full-time care to other kinds of dependents as well, including elderly Alzheimer's patients, invalids, and severely retarded people. Such caregivers, she argues, perform a valuable service for society as well as for the dependents. Such a program may even save society money, since it is cheaper to support one willing caregiver than to house someone in a nursing home or other care facility.[5]

Force AFDC Parents to Work?

According to Professor Eveline M. Burns, one original purpose of government aid to families with dependent children was so "that the mother would not have to seek employment and thus would be able to remain at home and provide care for her children." In a sense, it was even designed to persuade them to stay home. Even then, however, "the payments [were] almost nowhere adequate enough to remove all inducement to the mother (and sometimes the children) to seek paid employment."[6]

Today, the emphasis is almost reversed. The current governmental view was expressed by President Bush when he declared that people who receive aid today have "a responsibility to seek work, education or job training."[7] In line with this philosophy, several states have introduced measures, sometimes called "Workfare" to pressure AFDC mothers to find work.

The federal government has moved both to make this easier for the states to do, and to force them to do it, with the federal Family Support Act. This measure requires every state to provide a Job Opportunities and Basics Skills (JOBS) program for AFDC parents. The JOBS program is designed to train unemployed AFDC parents in the skills they need to get and hold a job.

The training will not be entirely voluntary. The federal government has goals for the states, requiring them to include at least 7 percent of all employable adults in the JOBS program by 1990, and 20 percent by 1995. Federal funds for the program will be reduced in any state that doesn't meet these goals.

In addition to work training for older parents, many states are requiring teenaged mothers who do not have high school diplomas to go back to school.

The main purpose of these programs is to enable—or to force—as many families as possible to get off AFDC. The Congressional Budget Office estimates that at least 51,000 families will be removed in the first five years. This is expected to save AFDC about $4 billion, more than $3 billion of it in federal money.[8]

In other ways, however, AFDC rules make it harder for parents to work. Typical AFDC parents have no one to look after their children when they go to work. The kinds of jobs generally available to them don't pay enough to afford daycare. What is more, any money they earn at their job is deducted from their AFDC benefit. This means that most parents would actually *lose* money by going to work at a low-paying job. Worse, they would lose their eligibility for Medicaid, leaving them unable to pay for medical care if they or one of their children got sick.

The Family Support Act tries to overcome these problems. It requires the states to provide twelve months of child care, six months of Medicaid, and six more months of other medical help for AFDC recipients who lose their benefits because they go to work. The president asked for $1.369 billion for AFDC work programs and child care in 1991. The Congress provided even more.

In practice, however, the promised help is often unavailable. According to an ABC News report, only 2.5 percent of the poor families in Franklin, Ohio, get any financial help for daycare.[9] Even where money *is* readily available, it is sometimes useless. No amount of aid can help a family get daycare where there is no daycare to be found. What a Massachusetts AFDC mother told a television interviewer in 1988 is still true in many places: "[They] say that they provide daycare, and they don't provide daycare. They provide you with a sheet of paper with listings of daycares. If there's not a space, then you know, you just have to keep looking."[10] In Columbus, Ohio, for instance, there are 500 children on a waiting list for a single daycare center for poor children.[11]

Tie AFDC Benefits to Education?

Much of the national AFDC debate has centered around several key reforms to AFDC that have already been tried experimentally on the state level. These include Wisconsin's Learnfare program, which ties a family's AFDC benefits to the children's daily attendance at school. Wisconsin's program is very strict; benefits are cut after only three days of unexcused absence in a single month.

Learnfare is popular with politicians, who argue that the need for school attendance is obvious. Education is the only real pathway most poor children have to take them out of poverty.

Many AFDC parents object to Learnfare, however. They argue that it is unfair to cut a family's desperately needed support because of one child's misbehavior. Parents often find it difficult to keep track of their children when they are away from home. Besides, they point out, there might be a good reason for a child to refuse to go to school. Students who attend gang-ridden inner-city schools are often afraid to go when trouble is brewing there. And, in any case, they say, even a child who disobeys and plays hooky still needs to be fed and clothed.

So far, the results of the Learnfare experiment have been controversial. The state administration of Governor Tommy Thompson, which introduced Learnfare, claims it is a success. A research study commissioned by the state casts doubt on these claims, however. It found that the attendance records of 36 percent of the children whose families' benefits were cut during the first year of the program did improve. But the attendance records of over 50 percent actually got worse.[12] The Thompson administration was so displeased that it fired the research firm it had hired to do the study.[13]

Ohio's Project Learn is designed to convince teenage parents to continue their own education. It adds a $62 bonus to a family's AFDC benefit if a teenage parent is in school, or cuts the benefit by the same amount if he or she is not. Some critics complain that $62 is too little even to provide care for the child (or children) while the parent is at school.

Other major demonstration projects combine several existing programs into one, or combine them with new programs in interesting ways. The state of Washington's Family Independence Program, for example, combines food stamps and AFDC benefits into one cash grant, and then adds incentive payments for recipients who get job training or go to work. Minnesota's Family Investment Plan involves several measures that combine AFDC and food stamps for certain families, or combine food stamps, Medicaid, and help with child care into a package for certain others who don't qualify for AFDC itself.

A more drastic suggestion is to replace AFDC with a mandatory refundable child care credit. This would provide a tax refund to all parents of young children to allow them to provide for their care. Because it would be both "mandatory" and "refundable" it would be automatically paid to poor parents, whether they actually pay any taxes or not. This is along the lines of programs in Canada, and several other western countries, that provide grants to all parents of young children regardless of income.

Reduce Benefits for "Extra" Children?
In April, 1992, President Bush announced that his administration was giving the state of Wisconsin permission for a new experiment. For the next five years, Wisconsin would be free to cut benefit increases to families who

have children while receiving AFDC. Wisconsin Governor Tommy Thompson, who proposed the plan, announced that it would be tried out in four Wisconsin counties, including the one containing the state's biggest city, Milwaukee.

Under the plan, single welfare mothers in those counties will receive only half the usual benefit increase for their first new child, and no increase at all for any children after that. California and New Jersey are apparently considering similar laws.

Besides saving money, the purpose of these reforms is to pressure women already on AFDC not to have children. Some supporters of the plan argue that welfare mothers look upon having children as a way of increasing their incomes. When they no longer get "extra" money for "extra" children, the plan's supporters say, women will think twice about having them. When asked if there is any evidence that current welfare mothers actually do have more children in order to receive more benefits, Governor Thompson admitted that, "There really isn't. But," he added, "there is no evidence to the contrary, either."[14]

The Child Welfare League of America protests that the Wisconsin plan "will end up hurting the very children we seek to help."[15] The more children a family has, the more money it needs to provide for them. That need doesn't change because a family is receiving AFDC. A child born to a welfare mother deserves food, clothing and shelter as much as a child born to someone else, the critics insist. To punish children for being born "on welfare" is not only unfair, but cruel. Other critics argue that this policy may encourage poor women to have abortions, rather than face the prospect of having another mouth to feed with no help from the government.

National Health Insurance

By far the biggest unresolved welfare issue in the United States today is the question of national health insurance.

No issue is of more concern to more people, and no issue goes deeper to the heart of America's future as a welfare state.

As we have seen, health coverage is usually one of the first programs introduced in a welfare state. Yet, the United States remains the only country in the developed world that does not provide some system of national health insurance for its people.

The issue has been lurking in the background of American politics at least since President Truman proposed national health insurance after World War II. In recent years it has come to the fore, thanks to skyrocketing health care costs that have made it impossible for most Americans to pay their own health care bills in the event of a long-term illness.

In 1991, a major private health insurance company study predicted that in the future health care costs would eventually bankrupt almost everyone who lives long enough to retire.[16]

Those Americans who can do so purchase health insurance from private companies. But millions of Americans cannot find a company to insure them because they already have a health problem. Millions more simply cannot afford private insurance, although they are not poor enough to qualify for Medicaid. It is estimated that roughly 50 million Americans have no health insurance at all.[17]

As we have seen, the U.S. government already plays a major role in providing health care through Medicare and Medicaid. But that care is restricted to the old, the poor, and the disabled. Until now, the fear of higher taxes and "socialized medicine" has been enough to head off calls for a broader national insurance plan. But that may be changing.

There is a growing agreement that something has to be done. The old resistance to the idea of national health insurance is crumbling fast. In a recent television interview, Senate Majority Leader George Mitchell spoke of the "principle that good health care is a right . . . not a privilege [only] for those who can afford it."[18] Most Americans seem to agree with him. A 1991 public opinion poll, commissioned by two major news organizations, showed that 70 percent of Americans favored government-paid health insurance for people who cannot afford to buy their own. Even more significantly, 67 percent favored government-paid insurance for all Americans, whether they could afford private insurance or not.[19]

Most Americans find it hard to accept the idea that health care should be either charity or a luxury. Medicare takes care of the old. Medicaid takes care of the poor. The rich can take care of themselves. But who, or what, will take care of the middle class?

Many ideas have been proposed. One is that the government should require all employers to provide health insurance for their employees, as some already do. Opponents of this idea protest that it would bankrupt many small businesses, and still leave millions of the unemployed and the self-employed without coverage.

The most conservative reformers argue that the government should do no more than plug the holes in the private insurance system that already exists. At most, they say, it could help pay for private coverage for those who are unable to get insurance on their own.

Representative Pete Stark (Dem.-Calif.) has suggested expanding Medicare to cover everyone.[20] This has the advantage of being relatively simple, but opponents argue that it would be like fitting an immense round peg into a small square hole. Besides, they point out, Medicare only pays for a portion of the care many people actually need.

A more ambitious idea is to start over with a single new national insurance scheme that would cover virtually all medical expenses. One version of this plan calls for it to be funded by a separate payroll tax like that for Social Security.

Whatever plan is adopted is bound to cost the government—that is, the taxpayers—an enormous amount of money. Conservatives believe that any government plan is likely to push already high health care costs even higher. The government, they say, is inevitably inefficient. A great deal of money is bound to be wasted, and that will force overall costs upward.

More optimistic reformers suggest that the actual costs of providing health care will only rise a little, or not at all, under government health insurance. All it would do, they say, is simply channel all money now being spent privately through a single payer, the federal government.

Some even claim that national health insurance would save overall health expenses. A single system would be much cheaper to administer than the hundreds of separate insurance systems (including Medicare and Medicaid) we have today. What's more, since the government would be paying virtually all the bills, it would be able to dictate how much it would pay for various medical services.

There is no agreement yet about what kind of insurance system the United States should have. But it seems clear that some kind of national system will be adopted soon. Whatever it turns out to be, it will confirm America's position as a welfare state.

The Future of the American Welfare State

In the 1980s, the American welfare state underwent the most powerful political attack ever mounted against it. An enormously popular conservative president, Ronald Reagan, did everything he could to undermine and dismantle it. And yet, the welfare state has survived. In fact, in one extremely important area, that of health insurance, it seems to be expanding.

The attack on the welfare state may or may not be continued during the rest of the 1990s and beyond. There are bound to be many reforms of the welfare system over that time. Some will strengthen it, some will weaken it. But it seems certain that the welfare state will continue to survive.

The cost of maintaining the welfare system is enormous. But the cost of abandoning it would be even higher. It would mean abandoning a fundamental commitment that the American people have made to themselves.

That commitment is founded upon the Constitution's call to "promote the General Welfare," but that commitment is constantly being reshaped and redefined. That is because the definition of what constitutes the general welfare is constantly being reshaped and redefined. Most Americans would now agree that it includes some minimum standard of living for all citizens, but what that minimum should be will continue to be the subject of great debate.

What New York Senator Herbert H. Lehman said more than forty years ago is still true today: "We are still far from the goal we seek. Insecurity still haunts millions. Inadequate housing poisons the wells of family life in vast numbers of cases. Inadequate schooling handicaps a great segment of our people. And the fear of sickness and old age still clutches at the hearts of many if not most of our fellow citizens. Until we solve all these problems and quiet all these fears, our people will not be truly free."[21]

Source Notes

CHAPTER ONE
What Is a Welfare State?

1. Sam Fullwood III, "Census Bureau Says 1 in 7 are Now Living in Poverty," *Los Angeles Times*, September 27, 1991.
2. Don Williamson, "Attack Homelessness at its Root," *The Atlanta Journal and Constitution*, January 1, 1991.
3. Interviewed on *CNN Headline News*, October 10, 1991.
4. Fullwood.
5. Suggested by the Families USA Foundation and the Center on Budget and Priorities, and reported in "Our Impoverished Millions," *Miami Herald*, October 21, 1990.
6. "We Must Attack and Defeat Child Poverty," *CDF Reports*, January/February, 1991, p. 2.
7. "New Report Examines Homelessness Among Children and Families," *CDF Reports*, April 1991, p. 3.
8. Vee Burke, *Welfare*, A Congressional Research Service Issues Brief, Congressional Research Bureau, Library of Congress, updated October 18, 1990, p. 7.
9. Williamson.
10. Arthur Schlesinger, Jr., "The Welfare State," *Reporter*, October 11, 1949, p. 28.

CHAPTER TWO
"To Promote the General Welfare"

1. The Vanderbilts' comments are quoted in *American History: A Survey*, 4th ed., by Richard N. Current, T. Harry Williams, and Frank Freidel. (New York: Knopf, 1975), p. 465.
2. Darwin's theory was laid out in his book *Origin of Species*, available in the *Great Minds Series* (Buffalo: Prometheus Books, 1991). Darwin himself had nothing to do with the social theories that people like Carnegie tried to associate with his work.
3. Andrew Carnegie, "Wealth," *North American Review*, N. 148, June 1889. Reprinted in *Democracy and the Gospel of Wealth*,

Gail Kennedy, ed. (Boston: D.C. Heath and Company, 1949), p. 2.

4. Quoted by Marvin Olasky in "Lessons on Compassion: 19th-Century Welfare," *Policy Review*, Fall 1990. Reprinted in *Current*, February 1991, p. 9.

5. The Right Rev. William Lawrence, "The Relation of Wealth to Morals," *World's Work*, January 1901. Reprinted in *Democracy and the Gospel of Wealth* (Boston: D.C. Heath and Company, 1949), p. 69.

6. Charles S. Pierce, "Evolutionary Love," *The Monist*, January 1893. Excerpted as "The Century of Greed" in *Democracy and the Gospel of Wealth* (Boston: D.C. Heath and Company, 1949), p. 91.

7. Carnegie, p. 7.

8. Olasky, p. 8.

9. Current and others, p. 573.

10. For more on Jane Addams and her work, see Allen F. Davis's *American Heroine: The Life and Legend of Jane Addams* (New York: Oxford, 1973).

11. Ralph Henry Gabriel in "The Gospel of Wealth of the Gilded Age," *The Course of American Democratic Thought* (Ronald Press, 1940). Reprinted in *Democracy and the Gospel of Wealth* (Boston: D.C. Heath and Company, 1949), p. 61.

CHAPTER THREE
The Birth of the Welfare State

1. Harry K. Girvetz, "The Welfare State," *International Encyclopedia of the Social Sciences*. Reprinted in *Contemporary Western Europe*, Glenda G. Rosenthal and Elliot Zupnick, eds. (New York: Praeger, 1984), p. 32.

2. Ibid., p. 32.

3. Peter Flora and Jens Alber, "The Development of Welfare States in Europe," *The Development of the Welfare States in Europe and America*, edited by Peter Flora and Arnold J. Heidenheimer (New Brunswick, N.J.: Transaction Books, 1981). Reprinted in *Contemporary Western Europe*, Glenda G. Rosenthal and Elliot Zupnick, eds. (New York: Praeger, 1984), p. 274.

4. Girvetz, p. 33.

5. Jonathan Rose, "From Bismarck to Roosevelt: How the Welfare State Began," *Scholastic Update*, December 13, 1985, p. 13.

6. Ibid.

7. The outlines of the early development of welfare state programs in western Europe are based largely on Flora and Alber.

CHAPTER FOUR
The Development of the American Welfare State

1. Allan Nevins and Henry Steele Commager, *A Pocket History of the United States*, 7th ed. (New York: Washington Square Press, 1981), p. 416.
2. Richard N. Current, T. Harry Williams, and Frank Freidel, *American History: A Survey*, 4th ed. (New York: Knopf, 1975), p. 669.
3. Ibid., p. 655.
4. Ibid., p. 657.
5. Nevins and Commager, p. 416.
6. Fred J. Harris, *America's Democracy: The Ideal and the Reality* (Glenview, Illinois: Scott, Foresman, 1980), p. 94.
7. There are a great many books available on the New Deal and its efforts to relieve the Great Depression. Among the most recent is Anthony J. Badger's *The New Deal: The Depression Years* (New York: Hill & Wang, 1989).
8. Emmet John Hughes, "FDR: The Happiest Warrior," *Smithsonian*, April 1972, p. 33.
9. For the most powerful description available of what rural electrification meant, see Robert Caro's *The Path to Power: The Years of Lyndon Johnson* (New York: Knopf, 1982) pp. 502–526
10. Current and others, p. 741.
11. Nevins and Commager, p. 472.
12. Eveline M. Burns, "The Government's Role in Welfare," *The Nation's Children*, vol. 3, Eli Ginzberg, ed. (New York: Columbia University Press, 1960), p. 153.
13. Current and others, p. 793.
14. *The World Almanac and Book of Facts* (New York: World Almanac, 1990), p. 561.
15. *Chronicle of the 20th Century* (Mount Kisco: Chronicle Publications, 1987), p. 936.
16. Current and others, p. 796.
17. *Scholastic Update*, December 13, 1985, p. 4.
18. "Progress Against Poverty in the United States, 1959 to 1987," technical revision, 1990, a Congressional Research Service Report for Congress, Congressional Research Service, Library of Congress, Washington, D.C., p. 45.
19. Christopher Matthews, "Bush Does Little for Working Families," *The Arizona Republic*, September 2, 1991.
20. Don Williamson, "Attack Homelessness at its Root," *The Atlanta Journal and Constitution*, January 1, 1991.

21. Irving S. Shapiro, quoted in "Reforming Social Welfare Policy," *Children Today*, July-August 1989.

CHAPTER FIVE

Social Security: Foundation of the Welfare State

1. *HUD News*, U.S. Department of Housing and Urban Development, May 13, 1971, pp. 4–5.
2. "Fixing Social Security," *Newsweek*, May 7, 1990, p. 54. (Italics added by the author.)
3. "Understanding Social Security," a booklet published by the Department of Health and Human Services, Social Security Administration, Baltimore, January 1991, p. 7.
4. Ibid., p. 12.
5. "Medicare," a booklet published by the Department of Health and Human Services, Social Security Administration, Baltimore, May 1991, pp. 15–21.
6. "Understanding Social Security," p. 7.
7. "Retirement Security May Be an Illusion," *A Dream in Jeopardy*, published by the *Chicago Tribune*, Chicago, 1989, pp. 3–4.
8. "Workforce Drifts from Pension Coverage," ibid., p. 20.

CHAPTER SIX

Major Federal Welfare Programs

1. For a description of most federal welfare programs, see 89-595 EPW, *Cash and Noncash Benefits for Persons with Limited Income: Eligibility Rules, Recipient and Expenditure Data, FY 1986–1988*, available from the Congressional Research Service, Library of Congress, Washington, D.C.
2. Vee Burke, *Welfare*, A Congressional Research Service Issues Brief, updated October 18, 1990, p. 2.
3. "Understanding Social Security," a booklet published by the Department of Health and Human Services, Social Security Administration, Baltimore, 1991, p. 6.
4. Burke, p. 2.
5. George M. Anderson, "Old and Poor in the U.S.A.," *America*, November 3, 1990, p. 328.
6. Except where specifically stated otherwise, the welfare statistics cited in this chapter come from Burke.
7. Burke, p. 3.
8. "Aid to Families With Dependent Children," Division of Economic Support, Department of Health and Social Services, State of Wisconsin, undated, p. 6.

9. "Another Just Cause," *St. Petersburg Times*, March 26, 1991.
10. "Hunger in America," *CDF Reports*, April 1991, p. 4.
11. Ibid., p. 5.

CHAPTER SEVEN
Living on Welfare
1. "Hunger in America," *CDF Reports*, April 1991, p. 4.
2. Interviewed by the author, October 24, 1991.
3. Gowans interview.
4. "Letters to the Editor," *Wausau Daily Herald*, November 6, 1991.
5. Letter from Lillian Hanson, *Welfare Mothers' Voice*, Summer 1991, p. 4.
6. Kathryn Casey, "A Woman Today: This is Your Life," *Ladies Home Journal*, November 1991, p. 24.
7. Gowans interview.

CHAPTER EIGHT
The Welfare State Debate
1. Interviewed on the C-SPAN television network, June 11, 1991.
2. Vee Burke, *Welfare*, A Congressional Research Service Issues Brief, updated October 18, 1990, p. 3.
3. Sam Fullwood III, "Census Bureau Says 1 in 7 are Now Living in Poverty," *Los Angeles Times*, September 27, 1991.
4. Committee on Economic Policy of the Chamber of Commerce of the United States, *The Welfare State and the State of Human Welfare*, 1950. Quoted in *Liberals and Conservatives: a Debate on the Welfare State*, David L. Bender, ed. (Anoka, Minn.: Greenhaven Press, 1973), p. 85.
5. Juanita Kidd Stout, "Why Must the Taxpayers Subsidize Immorality?" *The Philadelphia Sunday Bulletin*, March 7, 1965.
6. Jack Kemp, Secretary of Housing and Urban Development, interviewed on C-SPAN, June 11, 1991.
7. From Goldwater's book, *Conscience of a Conservative*, Quoted in Bender, p. 25.
8. Burke, p. 2.
9. C-SPAN interview.
10. "The Unfinished War," *The Atlantic Monthly*, December 1988, p. 37.
11. Burke, p. 7.
12. Frances Fox Piven and Richard A. Cloward, *Regulating the Poor: The Functions of Public Welfare* (New York: Pantheon, 1971), p. i.
13. "Our Impoverished Millions: Lifting America's Poor and

Near-Poor Helps Us All," *The Miami Herald*, October 21, 1990.

14. The corporations are A.T.&T., Sky Chefs Inc., BellSouth Corp., Honeywell Inc., and The Prudential Insurance Company. Quoted in "Corporate America's Case for Women, Children," *St. Louis Post-Dispatch*, March 18, 1991.

15. Hubert H. Humphrey, "The Welfare State—A State of the General Welfare," *The Social Welfare Forum* (New York: Columbia University Press, 1950), excerpted in Bender, p. 36.

16. Ibid.

17. Thomas H. Walz and Beth Zemek, "The Upside Down Welfare State," an undated pamphlet published by the Minnesota Resource Center for Social Work Education. Reprinted in Bender, p. 71.

18. *Goldberg v. Kelly*, 397 U.S. 254, 90 S.Ct. 1011 (1970).

CHAPTER NINE
The Need for Reform

1. "Trying to Change Welfare," *Nightline*, ABC Television, September 20, 1988.

2. Reports before the 1990 Conservative Leadership Conference, and cablecast over the C-SPAN Television Network in November of that year.

3. *Welfare Myths vs. Facts*, a publication of the Department of Health, Education, and Welfare, quoted in *Liberals and Conservatives: a Debate on the Welfare State*, David L. Bender, ed. (Anoka, Minn.: Greenhaven Press, 1973), p. 90.

4. Representative Martha Griffiths, at a press conference on March 22, 1972. Her remarks were excerpted in Bender, p. 34.

5. George M. Anderson, "Old and Poor in the U.S.A.," *America*, November 3, 1990, p. 328.

6. "What It Takes: Structuring Interagency Partnerships to Connect Children and Families With Comprehensive Services," a monograph written for a consortium of Washington-based social service agencies, and political, social, and educational leaders. Quoted by William Raspberry in "Knit Social Services Into Seamless Web," *St. Louis Post-Dispatch*, February 5, 1991. Copyright 1991, by Washington Post Writers Group.

7. Raspberry.

8. "Hunger in America," *CDF Reports*, April 1991, p. 4.

9. "Tax Credits for Low-Income Families," *CDF Reports*, January/February 1991, p. 16.

10. Anderson, p. 329.
11. Senator Arlen Specter, interviewed on C-SPAN July 9, 1991.

CHAPTER TEN
Ideas for Reform

1. Olaf Palme, "In Praise of the Welfare State," a lecture first delivered at Harvard University's John F. Kennedy School of Government on April 8, 1984, reprinted in *Harpers*, August 1984, p. 22.
2. Ibid.
3. Report quoted in "America Earns an 'F' in Caring for Children," The Coos Bay, Oregon *The World*," March 13, 1990.
4. Ibid.
5. Gowans interview.
6. *The World.*
7. "Untangling the Welfare Mess," *Wausau Sunday Herald*, March 22, 1992.
8. Burke, p. 1.
9. *World News Tonight*, ABC-TV, June 19, 1991.
10. "Trying to Change Welfare," ABC-News *Nightline*, September 20, 1988.
11. *World News Tonight*, ABC-TV, June 19, 1991.
12. Results of the study reported on National Public Radio, *All Things Considered*, February 18, 1992.
13. Amy Rinard, "Evaluators Dumped in Learnfare Study," *Milwaukee Sentinel*, March 11, 1992.
14. "State Gets OK to Cut Welfare Payments," AP News story, *Wausau Daily Herald*, April 11, 1992.
15. Ibid.
16. "Retirement at Risk," a report prepared by the Northwestern National Life Insurance Company, described in "Retirees Facing 'Welfare Years,'" *USA Today*, November 14, 1991.
17. Testimony of Rep. Pete Stark before the House Ways and Means Committee, October 8, 1991.
18. Interviewed on *Today*, NBC-Television, August 16, 1991.
19. CNN/*Time* poll, reported by CNN-Television News, August 31, 1991.
20. Stark testimony.
21. Senator Herbert H. Lehman, "Freedom and the General Welfare," a speech delivered at the 45th Anniversary Conference of the League for Industrial Democracy on April 15, 1950. Printed in Bender, p. 52.

Bibliography

THE following books, reports, and articles give widely varying perspectives on the origins, history, and philosophy of the welfare state.

Books

Bender, David L., ed. *Liberals and Conservatives: A Debate on the Welfare State*, revised 3rd Edition. Anoka, Minn.: Greenhaven Press, 1982.

Cottingham, P.H., and D.T. Ellwood, eds. *Welfare Policy for the 1990s*. Cambridge: Harvard University Press, 1989.

Ellwood, David. *Poor Support*. New York: Basic Books, 1989.

Fine, Sidney. *Laissez-Faire and the General Welfare State: A Study of Conflict in American Thought*. Ann Arbor: University of Michigan Press, 1964.

Flora, Peter, and Arnold J. Heidenheimer, eds. *The Development of the Welfare States in Europe and America*. New Brunswick, N.J.: Transaction Books, 1981.

Friedman, Milton, and Rose Friedman. *Free to Choose: A Personal Statement*. San Diego: Harcourt Brace Jovanovich, 1990.

Friedman, Robert, and others, eds. *Modern Welfare States: A Comparative View of Trends and Prospects*. New York: New York University Press, 1987.

Harris, David. *Justifying State Welfare: The New Right Versus the Old Left*. Cambridge: Basil Blackwell, 1987.

Jansson, Bruce S. *The Reluctant Welfare State: A History of American Social Welfare Policies*. Belmont, Calif.: Wadsworth, 1988.

Kennedy, Gail, ed. *Democracy and the Gospel of Wealth*. Boston: D.C. Heath and Company, 1949.

Levitan, Sar A., and Clifford M. Johnson. *Beyond the Safety Net.* Cambridge: Ballinger, 1989.

Long, Robert Emmet, ed. *The Welfare Debate.* New York: H.W. Wilson, 1989.

Mead, Lawrence. *Beyond Entitlement.* New York: Free Press, 1985.

Morris, Robert, ed. *Testing the Limits of Social Welfare: International Perspectives on Policy Changes in Nine Countries.* Hanover, N.H.: University Press of New England, 1988.

Murray, Charles. *Losing Ground.* New York: Basic Books, 1986.

Piven, Frances Fox, and Richard A. Cloward. *Regulating the Poor: The Functions of Public Welfare.* New York: Pantheon, 1971.

Trattner, Walter I. *From Poor Law to Welfare State: A History of Social Welfare in America.* New York: Free Press, 1984.

Will, George. *Statecraft as Soulcraft.* New York: Simon & Schuster, 1983.

Reports, Magazine Articles and Other Publications

Anderson, George M. "Old and Poor in the U.S.A.," *America*, November 3, 1990.

Block, Walter. "Analyzing the Welfare System: The Excessive Influence of Government," *Vital Speeches of the Day*, March 15, 1989.

Burke, Vee. "Welfare." A Congressional Research Service Issues Brief, Congressional Research Bureau, Library of Congress, Washington, D.C., 1990.

"Cash and Noncash Benefits for Persons with Limited Income: Eligibility Rules, Recipient and Expenditure Data, FY1986–1988." Congressional Research Service, Library of Congress, Washington, D.C., 1989.

Drew, Christopher, and Michael Tackett. *A Dream in Jeopardy*, a series of articles originally published in *The Chicago Tribune*, December 3 through December 10, 1989, and published separately under this title later in the year.

Greenstein, Robert. "Losing Faith in 'Losing Ground,'" *The New Republic*, March 25, 1985.

Lemann, Nicholas. "The Unfinished War," *The Atlantic Monthly*, December 1988.

Olasky, Marvin. "Lessons on Compassion: 19th Century Welfare," *Policy Review*, Fall 1990.

Palme, Olaf. "In Praise of the Welfare State," a lecture first delivered at Harvard University's John F. Kennedy School of Government on April 8, 1984, reprinted in *Harpers*, August 1984.

Rose, Jonathan. "From Bismarck to Roosevelt: How the Welfare State Began," *Scholastic Update*, December 13, 1985.
Schlesinger, Arthur, Jr. "The Welfare State," *Reporter*, October 11, 1949.

For the most direct and intensely felt perspective of all, however, interested readers could subscribe to the *Welfare Mothers' Voice*, which describes itself as "A paper by, for, and about AFDC mothers." It is published four times a year, in Milwaukee, Wisconsin (4504 N. 47th Street).

Index

Addams, Jane, 28
Aid to Families with
    Dependent Children
    (AFDC) program, 48,
    70–72, 104–5
Altruism, 38–39

Big Brother, welfare as, 84
Bismarck, Otto von, 35–36, 89
Bureaucracy, 77, 96
Burns, Eveline M., 104
Bush, George, 72, 83, 88, 96,
    104

Capitalism, 18–24, 33–34, 85
Carnegie, Andrew, 20, 22–25
Charity, 24–28, 60, 88–91
Children, 13–14, 72–73,
    80–81, 90, 103–4, 107–8
Children 1990: A Report Card,
    103
Civilian Conservation Corps,
    46
Classes, 18–20
Cloward, Richard A., 89
Commager, Henry Steele, 50
Communism, 35
Communist Manifesto, The, 34
Complexity, 97–98
Constitution, 17–18, 91–93
Coordination, 97–98
Corporations, 18–24

Costs of welfare, 83–84
Cucamonga, Rancho, 80

Darwinism, 20–24
Day care, 76, 105–7
Dependency, 99
"Deserving" poor, 28–30,
    101–2

Earned Income Tax Credits
    (EITC) program, 71, 98
Economic rights, 44–47,
    91–93
Education, 49, 51, 90, 106–7
Eisenhower, Dwight D., 50
Eligibility, 101–2
Ellwood, David, 95
Engels, Friedrich, 34
Europe, 31–38

Fair Deal, 49–50
Fair Labor Standards Act of
    1938, 46
Families, preservation of,
    99–100
Family Independence Program,
    107
Family Investment Plan, 107
Family Support Act, 104–5
Farmers, 33
Federal Emergency Relief
    Administration, 45

Financial protection, 59
Food stamps, 15, 51, 68, 73,
    80, 98
Fraud, 96, 100
Future, 111–12

Gabriel, Ralph Henry, 28
George, Lloyd, 37
Germany, 35–36
Girvetz, Harry, 33–34
Goals, reform, 99–100
Goldberg v. Kelly, 92
Goldwater, Barry, 86
Gospel of Wealth, The, 24–25
Gowans, Pat, 77, 79–81,
    103–4
Great Depression, 41–49
Great Society, 50–52, 88
Greenstein, Robert, 13

Head Start program, 51, 72
Health insurance, 37, 49,
    108–11
Homelessness, 13–14
Hoover, Herbert, 42, 44
Hopkins, Harry, 46
Housing, 49, 54, 68
Hull House, 28
Humphrey, Hubert, 91–93
Hyde, Floyd, 57

Immigrants, 26–27, 79
Industrialization, 18–19,
    32–34
Inefficiency, 95–98, 100
Infant mortality, 103
Initiative, 86
Inner city, 81

Job Corps, 51
Job Opportunities and Basic
    Skills (JOBS) program, 104
Johnson, Lyndon B., 50–52

Kemp, Jack, 83, 86–87

Laissez-faire, 21
Lawrence, William, 24, 28
Learnfare program, 106
Lehman, Herbert H., 112
Life on welfare, 75–82
Local programs, 74

Marx, Karl, 34, 39
Matthews, Christopher, 54
Means testing, 69, 73, 101–3
Medicaid, 15, 52, 70
Medicare, 15, 52, 61–64
Minimum wage, 46, 49
Misconceptions, 81–82
Mitchell, George, 109–10
Morality, 85, 101–2

National Labor Relations Act,
    46
National Youth
    Administration, 46
Natural selection, 22
Nevins, Allan, 50
New Deal, 43–49
Nixon, Richard, 52–53

Office of Economic
    Opportunity, 51
Opposition, 52–55, 83–88
Organized charity, 26–28

Palme, Olaf, 102–3
Pensions, 33, 35–37, 47–48,
    60–62, 64
Personal charity, 25–26
Pierce, Charles S., 24
Piven, Frances Fox, 89
Poorhouses, 32
Poor Laws, 31–32, 89
Poverty, 13–14, 53–54,
    87–88, 99

Preamble, 17–18, 91
Prejudice, 19–24, 78–81
Privacy, 80, 84
Project Learn, 107
Protestant work ethic, 28

Quality of life, 90

Railroads, 18
Raspberry, William, 98
Reagan, Ronald, 53–55, 83,
    87–88, 96, 111
Reconstruction Finance
    Corporation, 43, 45
Reducing poverty, 99
Reform
    ideas for, 101–12
    need for, 95–100
Regulating the Poor, 89
Religion, 24–25
Rights, economic, 44–47,
    91–93
Robber barons, 20–21, 25
Rockefeller, John D., 20
Roosevelt, Franklin D., 43–44
Roybal, Edgar, 98
Rural charity, 25–26

Safety net, 60, 64
Salvation Army, 28
Schlesinger, Arthur, Jr., 15–16
Segregation, 50–51
Self-reliance, 86–87
Slums, 27, 49
Social Darwinism, 20–24, 83
Social Gospel, 24–25
Social insurance, 37
Socialism, 34–35, 85
Socialized medicine, 51, 109
Social programs, 15

Social Security, 15, 47–49,
    57–65
Specter, Arlen, 99
Stark, Pete, 110
Stigma, 78–81
Stock market crash, 41–43
Stout, Juanita Kidd, 86
Supplemental Security Income
    (SSI), 68–70
Survival of the fittest, 22

Taxation, 85–86
Tennessee Valley Authority, 46
Thompson, Tommy, 106, 108
Trap, welfare, 86–87
Truman, Harry S, 49, 52

"Undeserving" poor, 28–30
Unemployment insurance, 15,
    37, 48
Unions, 21
Urban poor, 26–28

Vanderbilt, Cornelius, 20–21
Vanderbilt, William, 21

War on poverty, 50–52, 87–88
Waste, 95–97, 100
"Welfare queens," 81, 96
Welfare Warriors, 77, 103–4
Well-being of society, 92
Workers, 33
    conditions for, 19, 33
    encouragement of, 99
    movements by, 35
    poor, 14
    protection for, 47
Workfare, 104
Workmen's compensation
    insurance, 48

About the Author

MICHAEL KRONEWETTER is a free-lance writer specializing in government, politics, and history. He is the author of seventeen other books, of which two of the most recent are *Covert Action* and *The New Eastern Europe*. Mr. Kronewetter lives in Wausau, Wisconsin, his hometown, with his wife and two children. He is active in amateur theater and writes an occasional column for the local newspaper.